THEMATIC UNIT

Gold Rush

Written by Nancy Bednar

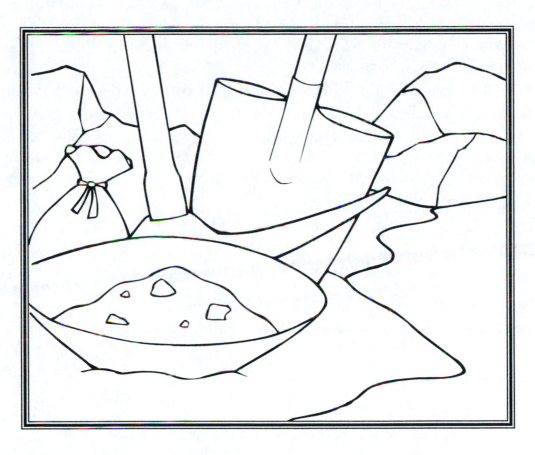

Teacher Created Materials, Inc.
6421 Industry Way
Westminster, CA 92683
www.teachercreated.com

©1994 Teacher Created Materials, Inc.
Reprinted, 2003

Made in U.S.A.
ISBN-1-55734-241-5

Edited by
Walter Kelly

Illustrated by
Agnes S. Palinay

Cover Art by
Keith Vasconcelles

Table of Contents

Introduction

Gold Rush contains a captivating whole language, thematic unit. Its 80 pages are filled with a wide variety of lesson ideas and activities designed for use with intermediate students. At its core are three high-quality children's literature selections, *Treasure in the Stream, Chang's Paper Pony* and *By the Great Hornspoon!* For each of these books, activities are included which set the stage for reading, encourage the enjoyment of the book, and extend the concepts gained. In addition, the theme is connected to the curriculum with activities in language arts, math, science, social studies, music, art, and life skills. Many of these activites encourage cooperative learning. Highlighted in this very complete teacher resource is a culminating activity which allows students to apply their knowledge of a time and place in history to present-day life.

This thematic unit includes the following:

- ☐ **literature selections**—summaries of three children's books with related lessons (complete with reproducible pages) that cross the curriculum

- ☐ **language experience, poetry, and writing ideas**—suggestions as well as activities across the curriculum

- ☐ **bulletin board ideas**—suggestions for student-created and/or interactive bulletin boards and displays

- ☐ **curriculum connections**—in language arts, math, science, social studies, life skills, music, and art

- ☐ **group projects**—to foster cooperative learning

- ☐ **a culminating activity**—which requires students to synthesize their learning to produce a product or engage in an activity that can be shared with others

- ☐ **a bibliography**—suggesting additional books on the theme

> To keep this valuable resource intact so it can be used year after year, you may wish to punch holes in the pages and store them in a three-ring binder.

Introduction *(cont.)*

Why Whole Language?

A whole language approach involves children in using all modes of communication: reading, writing, listening, observing, illustrating, experiencing, and doing. Communication skills are interconnected and integrated into lessons that emphasize the whole language rather than isolating its parts. The lessons revolve around selected literature. Reading is not taught as a separate subject from writing and spelling, for example. A child reads, writes (spelling appropriately for his/her level), speaks, listens, etc., in response to a literature experience introduced by the teacher. In this way, language skills grow naturally, stimulated by involvement and interest in the topic at hand.

Why Thematic Planning?

One very useful tool for implementing an integrated whole language program is thematic planning. By choosing a theme with correlative literature selections for a unit of study, a teacher can plan activities throughout the day that lead to a cohesive, in-depth study of the topic. Students will be practicing and applying their skills in meaningful contexts. Consequently, they tend to learn and retain more. Both teachers and students will be freed from a day that is broken into unrelated segments of isolated drill and practice.

Why Cooperative Learning?

Besides academic skills and content, students need to learn social skills. No longer can this area of development be taken for granted. Students must learn to work cooperatively in groups in order to function well in modern society. Group activities should be a regular part of school life, and teachers should consciously include social objectives as well as academic objectives in their planning. For example, a group working together to write a report may need to select a leader. The teacher should make clear to the students the qualities of good leader-follower group interactions and monitor them just as he/she would state and monitor the academic goals of the project.

Why Big Books?

An excellent cooperative, whole language activity is the production of Big Books. Groups of students or the whole class can apply their language skills, content knowledge, and creativity to produce a Big Book that can become a part of the classroom library to be read and reread. These books make excellent culminating projects for sharing beyond the classroom with parents, librarians, and others. Big Books can be produced in many ways, and this thematic unit book includes directions for several methods you may choose.

Treasure in the Stream

by Dorothy and Thomas Hoobler

Summary

Amy Harris lives on a little farm in Northern Califonia that her father leases from wealthy, powerful John Sutter. The story opens as Amy is about to make her first entry in her new diary on January 1, 1848. The quiet way of life her family has enjoyed soon comes to an end when gold is discovered at a mill being built by some of Mr. Sutter's workers along the American River. Even while news of the gold discovery is still a rumor, Amy struggles to keep a secret of her own—a nugget she discovered in the stream near her house. Amy's father has made it clear to the family that gold will only bring hundreds of miners that will ruin the land. She is faced with a dilemma: should she pan for gold herself, or tell her family and risk the peaceful way of life her family prefers? Amy finds out firsthand about the effects of gold fever when her secret gets out and her family is forced off their farm by hundreds of gold-hungry miners. Now her family must face a new challenge—life in San Francisco. The story ends with the Harris family successfully running a store started with the gold that Amy had found in the stream. The real treasure, of course, is her family and the love they have for each other.

The outline below is a suggested plan for using the various activitites that are presented in this unit. You should adapt these ideas to fit your own classroom situation.

Sample Plan

Lesson 1

- Introduce the unit with the Gold Rush Game, play it in cooperative groups, and then discuss. (pages 50-52)

- Read *Treasure in the Stream*.

- Work through the Discussion/Reflection Questions together. (page 8)

Lesson 2

- Do Gold in California! activity. (page 57)

- Make a Classroom Immigration Bar Graph together. (page 6)

- Discuss immigration and why it happens.

- Do Amy's Crossword Puzzle in cooperative groups to check reading comprehension. (page 9)

- Do Reading Response Journals. (page 10)

Lesson 3

- Set the mood and do Artistic Visualization activity. (pages 13, 14)

- Do Gold Rush Math activity. (page 56)

- Make Landforms relief maps. (page 65)

Lesson 4

- Do Amy's Time Line activity. (pages 15, 16)

- Do Family Traditions activity. (page 17)

- Make paper poppers. (page 17)

Lesson 5

- Make a class Big Book of the Gold Rush. (page 53)

- How to Pan for Gold activity. Discuss the methods and location. (page 71)

- Plan a gold mining expedition. (page 7)

Overview of Activities

Setting the Stage

---

1. Prepare a center for your classroom with several sets of the Gold Rush Game prepared according to directions. See page 50. Allow students to play the game several times, and then discuss the dangers and hardships of gold mining. An important discussion question might be, "How many people do you think really became rich by finding gold?"

2. Do Gold in California! activity on page 57. To extend this activity, paint some small pebbles, old game pieces, and some poker chips with gold paint. Ask students to weigh these items using a balance scale, and then find the "value" of each item at the gold rush value of $16.00 an ounce and today's market value.

3. Introduce the main character of the story—Amy Harris, a Swedish immigrant. In fact, everyone who lived in California in the 1840's (except the Native Americans) was an immigrant from somewhere. Ask students to share their family origins. Make a bar graph on poster board and display it in your classroom. Discuss immigration and why it happens.

Enjoying the Book

---

1. After reading *Treasure in the Stream*, do Discussion/Reflection Questions. Accept all reasonable answers and encourage students to share their opinions and ideas.

2. Do Amy's Crossword Puzzle in cooperative groups. This reading comprehension activity can become a competitive game or be used to work against the clock to find details in the story.

3. Doing the Reading Response Journal Activity will help students approach *Treasure in the Stream* as a piece of literature. Reproduce and distribute journal covers and pages.

   Put the answers to "What Do I Write?" (see page 10) on the board or overhead projector before you ask the students to choose a writing topic for their journals:

   > Have you ever had an experience like that?
   >
   > Have you ever felt that way? When? What happened?
   >
   > Do you agree or disagree? Why?
   >
   > What does this mean to you?

   Ask students to respond to a selected quotation from the story, or have them select one of their own.

Overview of Activities *(cont.)*

Enjoying the Book (cont.)

---

4. The Artistic Visualization activity is an art activity directly connected with the literature. Set the mood for this activity by reading the selected descriptions to students in a quiet, relaxed atmosphere, under dimmed lights if possible.

5. Amy's Time Line gives students an opportunity to put into historical perspective the events surrounding the California gold rush. To extend this activity, begin a discussion about the time differences between the discovery of gold and the arrival of the first gold seekers from the East Coast, about California statehood and the arrival of the first news of it in San Francisco, and about why Mexico would have given up California in the Treaty of Guadalupe Hidalgo one month after gold was discovered at Sutter's Mill.

6. Gold Rush Math: As the activity is completed by your students, discuss the importance of math skills in everyday life. Why would it have been important for a miner to have good math skills?

Extending the Book

---

1. Explore the multicultural aspects of the California gold rush with the Family Traditions activity on page 17. Directions for making a star string are contained in *Treasure in the Stream* after Chapter Five. Discuss ways of celebrating New Year's Day, and then construct a noisemaker to celebrate the differences and likenesses in your classroom!

2. To extend the familiarity with California that *Treasure in the Stream* provides to your students, look back at the varied geography of the state with the Landforms activity, page 65. Have on hand the materials to make relief maps: salt, flour, tempera, paint, brushes. Then allow the students the hands-on experience of forming mountains, oceans, and deserts.

3. Make a class Big Book of the California gold rush. Directions are on page 53. Each student should have his/her own page to display what he/she has learned about the gold rush and why it is of importance. This activity also incorporates cooperative learning—the groups need to complete the component parts of the book and assemble the completed product. Display the Big Book in the school library, office, or at Open House.

4. Distribute How to Pan for Gold directions to your students. Use the map on page 71 to decide on a likely place to look for gold. Read and discuss the directions carefully, and then plan a gold mining expedition. The plan should include travel methods and the time required, as well as equipment and supplies to be taken along.

Discussion/Reflection Questions

After reading *Treasure in the Stream*, discuss and answer the following questions about the story.

1. Do you think that the Harrises' ranch was successful? What parts of the story make you think so?

2. Everyone seemed to respect what Mr. Sutter had to say. Why do you think that was?

3. When the Harris family first arrived in California, it was part of Mexico. How had things changed in the past two years?

4. Who were the people who called themselves Californios?

5. When did Amy first hear about gold?

6. What did Amy's father think of the gold discovery at Mr. Sutter's mill?

7. How long was it from the time that Amy first heard about the gold discovery until the first miners from San Francisco arrived? Why do you think that was?

8. What happened to Mr. Sutter's land when the miners arrived?

9. Why did the Kutshers leave their farm and move south? Why was Amy's sister Sharon so sad?

10. Amy's mother had an idea for making money at the gold camps. What was it? Do you think it was a good idea?

11. When Amy showed the gold nugget to the Chinese miner, she knew she had made a mistake. What made her think so?

12. Who was Honest John? How would you describe him? What did he want from Amy?

13. Why did Amy decide to pan for gold in the stream? Why do you think she kept her mining a secret?

14. Everyone was surprised when Amy brought out the jars of gold she had found. What do you think her father thought?

15. Chapter Five tells what happened when the Harris family reached San Francisco. Describe what San Francisco was like.

16. Why did Amy's Father use some of the gold Amy found to buy something in San Francisco? What did he buy? Why did he buy it?

17. How did the Harrises' store get a reputation as a good place to buy?

18. Who was Levi Strauss? How did he become a wealthy man in California?

19. What happened on October 18, 1850? Describe the celebration. Why was everyone so happy?

Amy's Crossword Puzzle

Work in cooperative groups to solve this puzzle.

Go for the Gold! Can your group complete the puzzle first?

Check answers together.

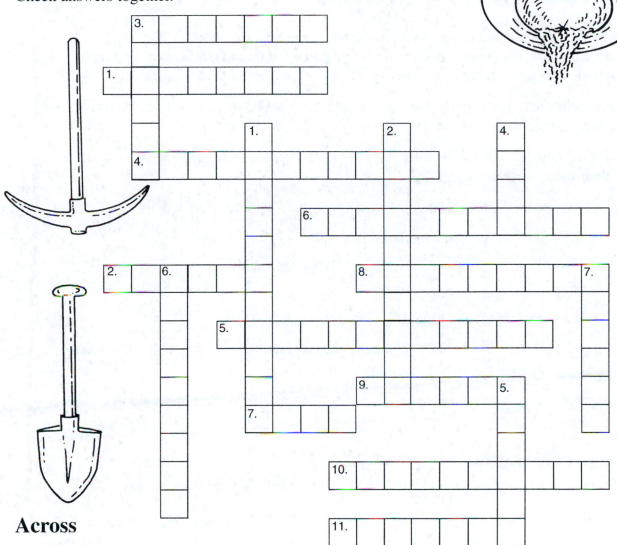

Across

1. "Cowboys" in California
2. What Amy found in the stream
3. Language spoken by most people in California in 1848
4. When Amy began her diary
5. Where Amy's family moved when they left the farm
6. Mexican people who remained in California after the war with the United States
7. What Amy's father bought in San Francisco
8. Broad-brimmed hats worn by vaqueros
9. What Amy's father did for a living
10. Important person expected for New Year's dinner

Down

1. Famous tailor the Harrises met in San Francisco
2. Place where Amy and her family lived
3. Amy's older sister
4. Amy's younger sister
5. Long ropes or lassos
6. Wanting gold so much that it becomes a sickness

Reading Response Journal

A Reading Response Journal provides students with an opportunity to explore a piece of literature by responding in their own words to a particular thought, quotation, or part of the action. Use these guidelines to help your students complete their journals.

1. Put a selected quotation on the board or overhead projector and ask students to copy it onto the left side of their journal page *exactly* as it is written.

2. Explain that the right side of the page is for their response, but ask them not to share their thoughts at this time.

3. Answer the inevitable "What do I write?" questions with answers like these:

   - Have you ever had an experience like that?

   - Have you ever felt that way? When? What happened?

   - Do you agree or disagree? Why?

   - What does this mean to you?

4. Any and all answers, spelling, punctuation, and grammar are acceptable. Reading Response Journals are never graded or corrected.

5. Students may share their Reading Repsonse Journals, but only if they care to volunteer.

Selected Quotations

You may want to use these quotations or have your students select others as they read.

"If the word spreads, it will bring hundreds of shiftless people up here. They'll be looking to get rich quick."

"So I can't tell anybody about the stone," she wrote in her diary. "It would make Father angry."

"She was ten years old, and definitely not a baby. She felt perfectly able to watch out for herself."

"She took her nugget out of her pocket. 'Is it gold?' she said. His eyes widened and right away she knew she had made a mistake."

Response Journal Cover

Use two-hole punch at top and secure pages with wire brads.

Response Journal Page

Use two-hole punch at top and secure pages with wire brads.

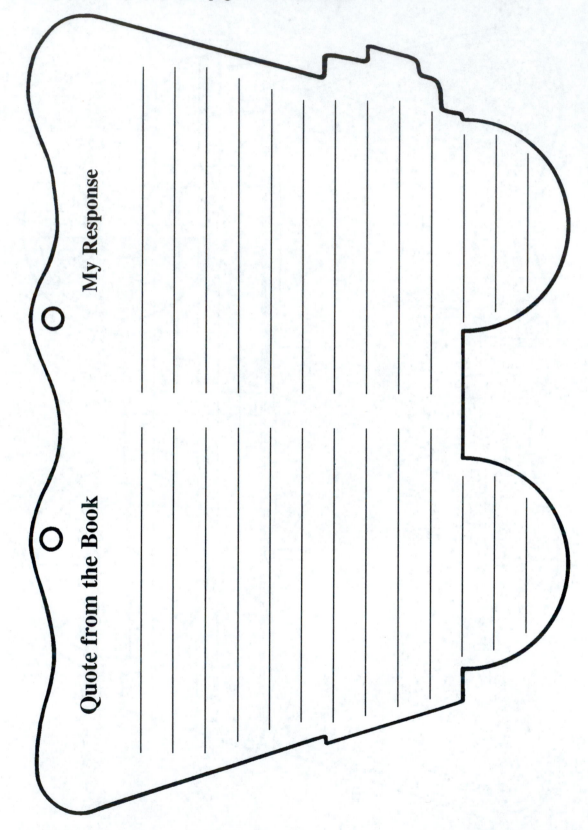

My Response

Quote from the Book

Artistic Visualization

Have you ever wondered where those terrific illustrations in your favorite books come from? Artists use the words in stories to make images of the characters and places in their minds. This is called visualization. Choose one of the descriptions from *Treasure in the Stream* to help you visualize your own illustration for the story and then draw it on the next page. Write a caption under your illustration to tell about it. Share the illustration with your class.

Descriptions:

Amy and little Fran went to the garden to pull carrots and turnips. Then they washed the dirt off in the stream that ran by the house. As they washed the vegetables, the sun reflected off a stone in the bottom of the stream. It looked pretty, and Amy picked it up and put it in her pocket. Maybe it would bring the family luck.

The fort came into sight. It was as big as a village. Only the roofs of the buildings showed above the high wooden walls. At the gate an American flag waved in the breeze.

One day a man with a mule stopped at the Harrises' house. He wanted to know where the gold was. 'None around here,' Father had told him firmly.

This man didn't look as if he had been too successful. His flannel shirt and heavy cotton pants were patched in places. He squatted barefoot in the stream, though most of the miners wore boots. His face looked thin.

She remembered where she had found the nugget. The stream curved just at that place, forming a pool where the water was clear. She took off her shoes and slid down the bank. A frog jumped into the water with a splash, stirring up the bottom sand.

Amy jumped out of bed and looked out the window. Dozens of men were digging up the land around their house!

The next morning Amy looked out of their window. It was wonderful how much you could see from up here. Hundreds of tents of all colors stood on the high hill beyond the hotel. Along the edge of the harbor there were wooden houses and stores, and dozens of men hard at work building more. And in the harbor itself were the black, bare masts of more ships than she could count.

At the parade that started at noon, everyone was carrying banners and wearing sashes of gold cloth. Soldiers marched in ranks, firing their rifles into the air. A group of Spanish Californios rode by on white horses. They were followed by the city's fire engines, pulled by horses decorated with flowers and streamers. Harbor workers pushed a small ship on wheels that they had built for the occasion. The Chinese people of the city tossed firecrackers and pinwheels into the streets.

Artistic Visualization *(cont.)*

Caption

_____

_____

_____

14

Amy's Time Line

Match the illustrations and dates on Amy's Time Line. Cut along the solid lines. Then glue the pictures and dates onto the blank time line on the next page in the order in which they happened.

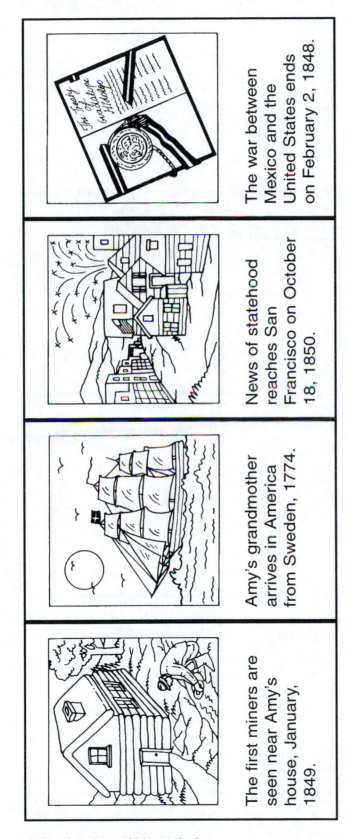

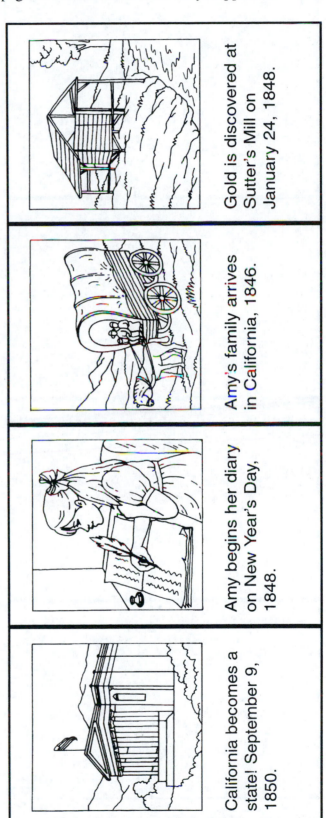

Amy's Time Line *(cont.)*

GLUE	

16

Family Traditions

Amy's family came to the United States from Sweden. In *Treasure in the Stream* Amy made a star string to decorate their house for a New Year's celebration.

Many cultures around the world believe that beginning a New Year with good food and good friends will help to guarantee having both in the year to come. They often celebrate such gatherings with gifts, parties, music, and noisemakers.

Did You Know . . . ?

- In Russia, "Grandfather Frost" gives children gifts on New Year's Day.
- In Vietnam, New Year's or Tet is celebrated sometime in January or February.
- In Austria, children receive a toy pig with a four-leaf clover in its mouth for luck.
- The Jewish culture celebrates Rosh Hashanah in September.

Activities

Write a short paragraph about New Year's or your favorite family holiday, and then share it aloud with the class.

Make a holiday popper for your next celebration. You will need a sheet of paper, 8 ½" x 11" (22 cm x 28 cm).

Holiday Popper

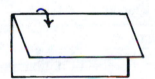

1. Fold the paper in half.

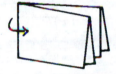

2. Fold it in half again.

3. Unfold the paper.

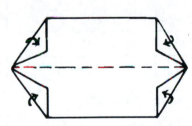

4. Fold the four corners so they meet on the horizontal line.

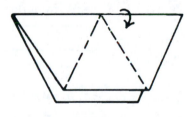

5. Then fold the paper in half lengthways.

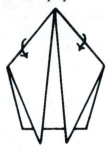

6. Now fold the two points down so the edges meet.

7. Then fold the paper back so that the section behind the pointed flaps is inside.

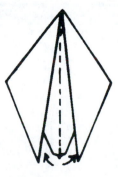

8. Now . . . hold the pointed flaps and snap your arm down quickly. The inside of the paper will snap out with a POP!

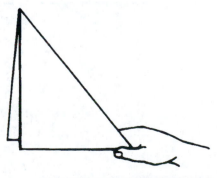

Chang's Paper Pony

By Eleanor Coerr

Summary

Chang's Paper Pony is the story of a boy and his grandfather who have fled wars and revolution in China to seek their fortune in "Gold Mountain," the name given to California by the Chinese. While Chang and his Grandpa Li endure the cruelty of prejudice from the miners in Gold Ditch, Chang's only friends are ". . . too old to play with." What Chang really wants is a pony as his friend, and he wants one with all his heart! When all seems lost, Chang's miner friend Big Pete comes through with an act of kindness and fair play that fulfills Chang's dream for a friend.

The outline below is a suggested plan for using the various activities that are presented in this unit. You should adapt these ideas to fit your classroom situation.

Sample Plan

Lesson 1

- Introductory Activity: The Chinese in California (page 19)
- Read *Chang's Paper Pony* aloud.
- Discussion/Reflection Questions (page 22)
- Interview Activity (page 22)
- Story Pyramid in cooperative groups (page 23)

Lesson 2

- Write Reader's Theater Script as a class activity. (page 24)
- Write a thank-you letter from Grandpa Li to Big Pete. (page 25)
- Construct a Friendship Pony. (page 26)

Lesson 3

- Chinese writing: Strokes and Characters (pages 27-29)
- Creative Writing (page 25)
- Reader's Theater Rehearsal

Lesson 4

- Construct a shoe-box diorama of a mining town. (page 25)
- Reader's Theater Dress Rehearsal
- Write a diary entry for Chang. (page 25)

Lesson 5

- Cooking Activity: Egg Rolls (page 30)
- Write a Chinese fortune. (page 25)
- Reader's Theater Presentation

Overview of Activities

Setting the Stage

---

1. Read and discuss The Chinese and the Gold Rush activity. Use the Chinese Calendar activity to promote interest in Chinese culture. Encourage students to research the Chinese calendar and Chinese culture in general in the school library and report on findings to the class.

2. Have students do a 5 to 10 minute Quick Write about a time when they have wanted something more than anything in the world.

   A Quick Write is a special kind of exercise that lets the students use the act of writing to discover what they already know. This works well if students write without planning and without looking back at what they have already written. When doing a Quick Write, students do not worry about spelling, punctuation, grammar, or even using complete sentences. The most important thing to do is to put down as many ideas as possible on their papers. After the Quick Write, students complete the activity by editing their work with a study-buddy and rewriting the work in standard English. Students usually want to share their work by reading their Quick Writes aloud.

3. Conduct a class discussion about the Chinese in California during the gold rush. Accept all ideas. Make an "Idea Web" on a large piece of butcher paper to be shared again after reading *Chang's Paper Pony.*

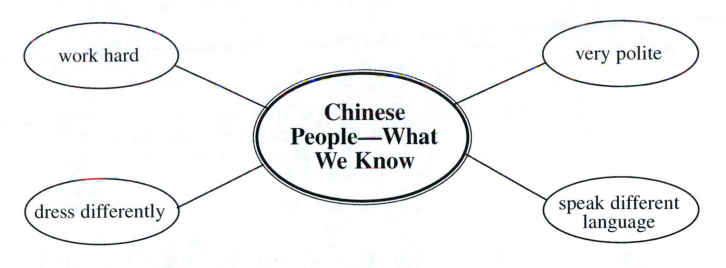

Enjoying the Book

---

1. Read the book aloud in class. Allow time for student reaction and discussion of the story as you read.

2. Do a role-playing Interview Activity on page 22 to explore the characters' feelings in the story.

3. Following guidelines on page 24, have students write a Reader's Theater adaptation of the book.

Overview of Activities *(cont.)*

Enjoying the Book (cont.)

4. Use the Story Pyramid activity on page 23 to help students identify the elements of a story—setting, characters, plot, and action. Then use the pyramid to construct a short story.

5. Ask students to pretend that they are Grandpa Li from the story. Discuss Grandpa Li's feelings, and then have students write a thank-you letter from Grandpa Li to Big Pete.

6. Explore Chang's likes and dislikes and what he really wants most; have students write a diary entry for a typical day for Chang in Gold Ditch. Read the entries aloud in class.

Extending the Book

1. Chinese writing is an ancient art form as well as a means of communication. Use the Chinese Strokes and Characters activities on pages 27-29 to expand the students' appreciation of the written word. After practicing, have students write a short story using as many Chinese characters as possible in place of words. Display the stories in the classroom.

2. Rehearse and perform the Reader's Theater as a class. Invite parents or other classrooms to attend your performance.

3. Use math skills to expand a recipe for egg rolls on page 30 as a treat for your class. This cooking activity is not only a practical application of math skills, but it can also be used as a lesson in hospitality if you plan to serve the egg rolls at your performance of the Reader's Theater.

4. As a creative writing activity, have students write a fortune for someone they do not know. Fortunes should consist of a good thought for the day, an element of wisdom, or a saying that they have heard. These can be distributed to the audience at the performance of the Reader's Theater.

5. Construct a mining town diorama from a shoe box. This can be done individually or as a cooperative group project.

The Chinese and the Gold Rush

When the first Chinese merchants arrived in San Francisco, they were looked upon as a real asset to the city. They were looked up to for being honest, orderly, and efficient businessmen. After 1850, however, prejudices against "foreigners" in California became so bad that the Chinese immigrants, who were not protected by laws, were badly mistreated in the gold camps.

As more people crowded into the gold camps, it became more and more difficult to find the riches they were all after. It did not take long for the white American citizens to decide that foreigners of all kinds were not entitled to the gold found on American soil.

In 1850, there were only a few hundred Chinese people in California. Two years later there were over 20,000. To protect themselves against the prejudice of the American miners, the Chinese often worked together in their own camps. Some of the Chinese who had gold mining experience in places like Borneo and Malaysia were able to extract gold from claims with such devices as the "Chinese Waterwheel." The Chinese worked very hard, but their success just made the prejudice worse. Soon there were laws such as "John Chinaman" and "heathen" laws forbidding foreigners from mining in many districts.

Questions

1. How were the Chinese thought of when they first arrived in San Francisco?
2. What do you think was responsible for the miners' prejudice against the Chinese?
3. What did the Chinese miners do to protect themselves in the gold camps?
4. Why did the laws not protect the Chinese miners in the gold camps?

Did You Know...?

The Chinese calendar is the oldest continually used calendar in the world. As of 1994, it will be 4,692 years old!

The Chinese calendar is made up of cycles of 12 years. Each of the 12 years is named after an animal.

If you were born in the year of the Dog, you are said to be honest and loyal. If you were born in the year of the Ox, you are patient and kind.

Check the Chinese calendar to find when you and your friends and family members were born. Do the animal signs match their personalities?

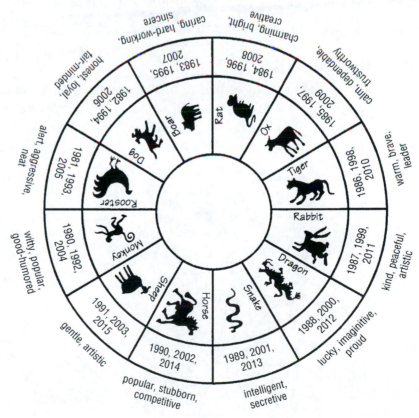

Discussion/Reflection Questions

Read *Chang's Paper Pony* aloud in class. After reading, do the following questions together.

1. What did Chang want most in the world?

2. Chang and his grandfather were not treated well by some of the miners. Why do you think this was?

3. What were some of the reasons Grandpa Li gave for the miners' poor behavior?

4. Do you think Chang was a good student?

5. If you knew only Chinese, do you think it would be fun to learn English? Why?

6. How was Big Pete different from the other miners? Why? Describe Big Pete.

7. How do you think Chang felt when Big Pete agreed to take him mining?

8. Do you think Chang had Gold Fever? Why?

9. What happened when Chang kept his promise to clean Big Pete's cabin?

10. Were you surprised by the ending of the story?

11. Do you think any of the other miners would have treated Chang as Big Pete did? Why?

Interview Activity

Divide the class into groups of three. In each group of three students, one student will be a newspaper reporter and the other two students will be miners. The reporter will question the miners about their feelings regarding "foreigners" in the gold camps. Students will take turns at these roles, write the results of their interviews, and share their findings aloud with the rest of the class.

Story Pyramid of
Chang's Paper Pony

Choose words carefully to complete the pyramid. Work together in cooperative groups to make good choices.

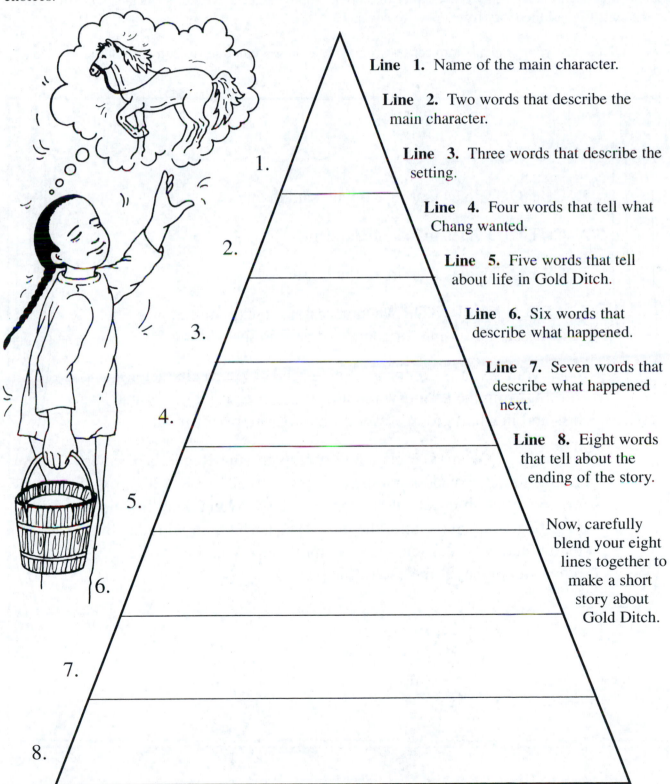

Line 1. Name of the main character.

Line 2. Two words that describe the main character.

Line 3. Three words that describe the setting.

Line 4. Four words that tell what Chang wanted.

Line 5. Five words that tell about life in Gold Ditch.

Line 6. Six words that describe what happened.

Line 7. Seven words that describe what happened next.

Line 8. Eight words that tell about the ending of the story.

Now, carefully blend your eight lines together to make a short story about Gold Ditch.

©

Reader's Theater

Reader's Theater is a performance of a book or a story, using only the voices of the actors to create the setting, action, and characters of the play.

An entire book can be adapted for Reader's Theater if it is relatively short (e.g., *Chang's Paper Pony*). Usually it is best to adapt only one chapter of a book, hoping that the Reader's Theater will stimulate the students to read the story from cover to cover.

Now . . . let's turn your students into script writers! Use these guidelines to convert your story into a script.

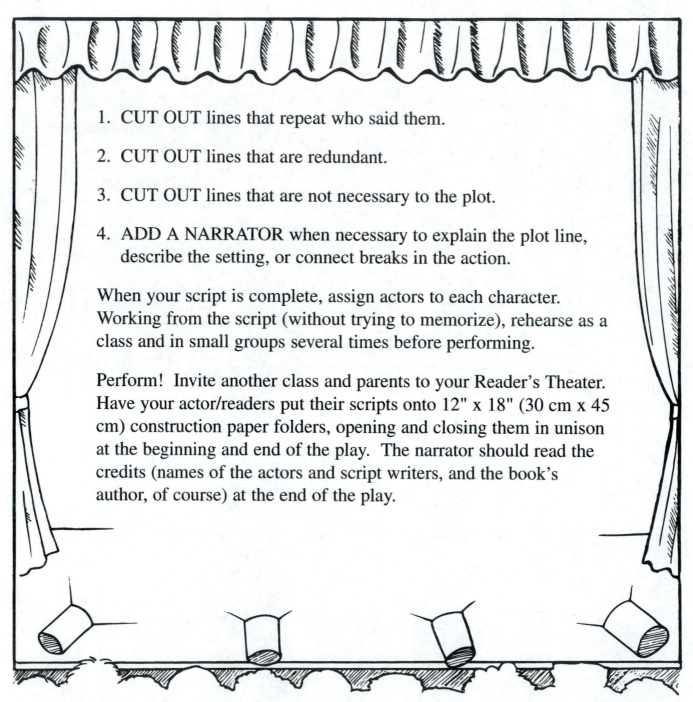

1. CUT OUT lines that repeat who said them.

2. CUT OUT lines that are redundant.

3. CUT OUT lines that are not necessary to the plot.

4. ADD A NARRATOR when necessary to explain the plot line, describe the setting, or connect breaks in the action.

When your script is complete, assign actors to each character. Working from the script (without trying to memorize), rehearse as a class and in small groups several times before performing.

Perform! Invite another class and parents to your Reader's Theater. Have your actor/readers put their scripts onto 12" x 18" (30 cm x 45 cm) construction paper folders, opening and closing them in unison at the beginning and end of the play. The narrator should read the credits (names of the actors and script writers, and the book's author, of course) at the end of the play.

Creative Writing

✏️ Write a thank-you letter from Grandpa Li to Big Pete. (What would Grandpa Li say to Big Pete to thank him for his kindness, fairness, and understanding?)

✏️ Write a diary entry for Chang. (What do you think Chang's days were like? What did he do? Who were his friends? Do you think he liked school?)

✏️ Write a "Chinese Fortune"— a good thought, an element of wisdom, or a happy saying. Have the students take turns reading them aloud in class, making sure there are no duplications. Then rewrite them on 2" x 4" (5 cm x 10 cm) pieces of red paper. (Red is for good luck!) Have each student give a good-luck fortune to a guest at the class performance of the Reader's Theater for *Chang's Paper Pony*.

Mining Town Diorama

Art Connection

Construct a shoe-box diorama of a gold town. Include miners' camps, staked-out claims, and various mining techniques.

Friendship Pony

While Chang played with his paper pony, he dreamed of having a real friend. After constructing the paper pony, use it to share your ideas of friendship with the class. Complete this sentence as many times as you can on your paper pony: A friend means . . . .

Directions:

Cut your pony out carefully. Then fold on the dashed lines in the following order, matching the numbers on the illustration.

1. Fold in half lengthways and then unfold.
2. Fold back.
3. Fold back and unfold.
4. Fold back.
5. Fold back and unfold
6. Fold up.
7. Fold up.
8. Cut tail strips. Fold down. Reinforce. Fold in the order first folded. Form horse figure.

Display your Friendship Pony on your desk.

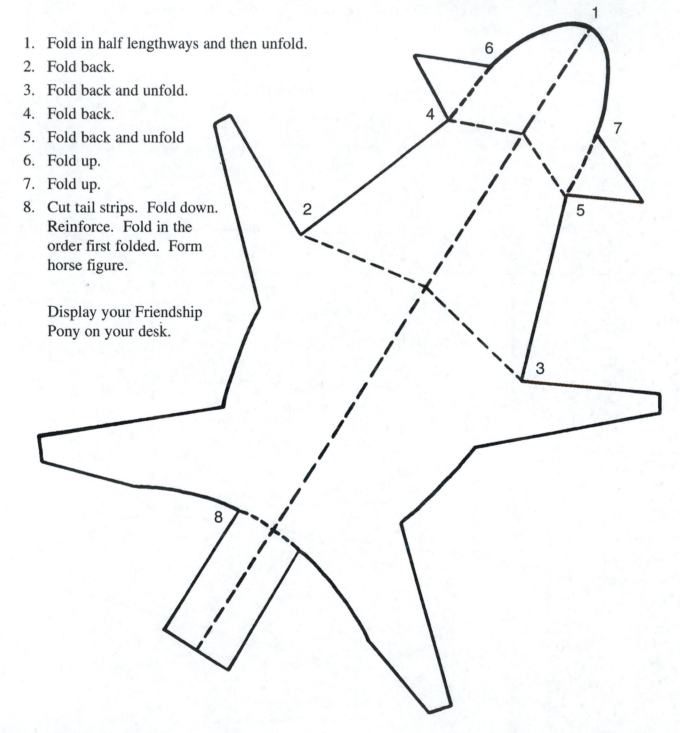

Chinese Writing

In *Chang's Paper Pony,* Chang had a real problem learning how to read and write in English. The words on a page looked to him like worms wiggling across the paper.

It must have been very difficult for Chang to learn English. English is very different from Chinese. Both languages are written with symbols. In English, the symbols stand for the sounds of the words when we say them out loud. In Chinese, the symbols represent a picture of what the word is.

These Chinese writing symbols are called *characters.* The Chinese have been using characters to represent words for more than 5,000 years.

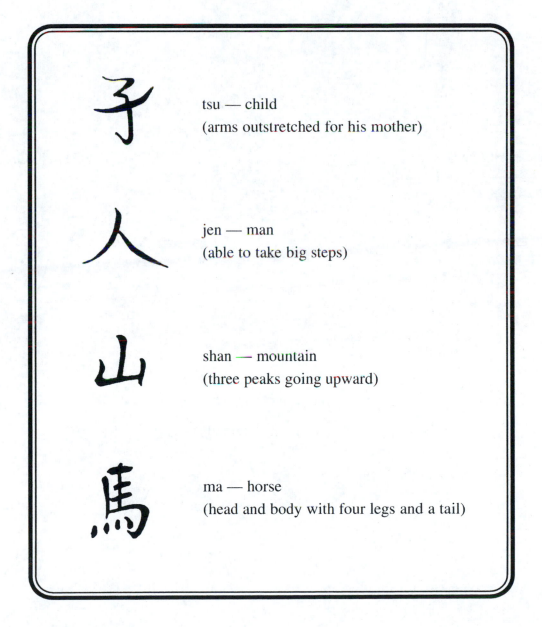

tsu — child
(arms outstretched for his mother)

jen — man
(able to take big steps)

shan — mountain
(three peaks going upward)

ma — horse
(head and body with four legs and a tail)

27

Chinese Writing Strokes

All Chinese characters are drawn with a few basic strokes. Practice drawing these a few times before you start to write the characters. Always draw the strokes from the top down and from left to right.

STRAIGHT LINES   ANGLED LINES   CURVES

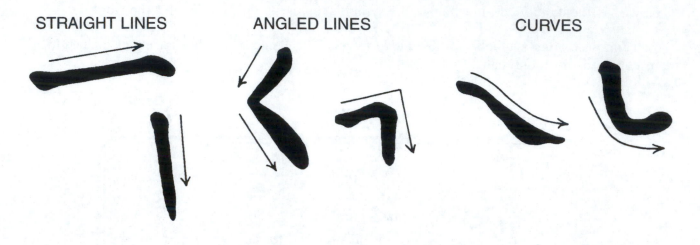

LINES WITH HOOKS   CURVES WITH HOOKS

SHORT STROKES

(some slant differently)

Writing Chinese Characters

Always draw the strokes in the same direction.

Always draw them in the order in which the arrows are numbered.

Practice the strokes and characters, and then write a short story using as many Chinese characters as you can in place of words.

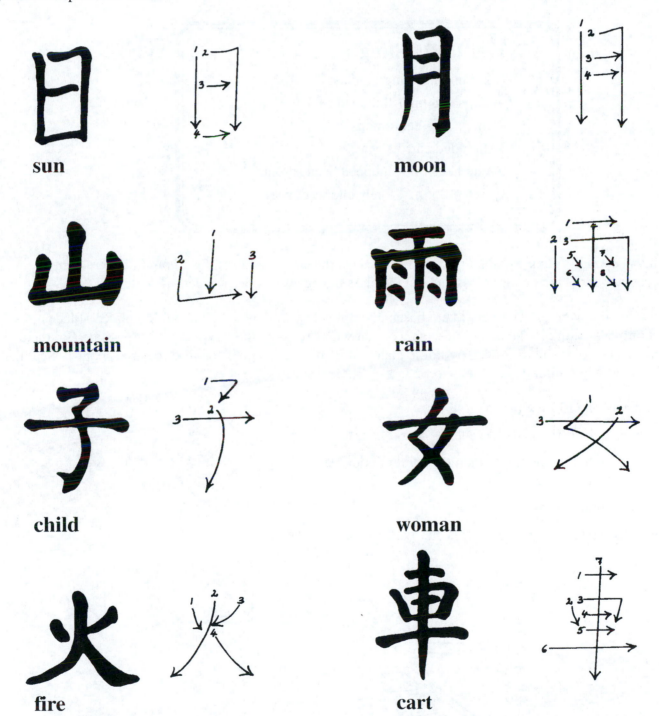

sun   **moon**

mountain   **rain**

child   **woman**

fire   **cart**

Chinese Cooking: Egg Rolls

Egg rolls can be prepared together in class, using an electric skillet. (Be very, very careful with hot oil!) Prepared won ton wrappers are available at most supermarket deli counters or at Chinese grocery stores.

Prepare filling ahead of time; have your students measure ingredients.

Egg Roll Filling

Combine these ingredients:

³/₄ cup (188 mL) shredded cabbage

2 chopped green onions

1 shredded carrot

¹/₂ cup (125 mL) chopped bean sprouts

¹/₂ cup (125 mL) finely chopped celery

This is enough filling for about 12 egg rolls. Have the class calculate the amount of ingredients necessary for (1) the entire class and (2) the class plus guests at the Reader's Theater.

Arrange the won ton wrappers like a baseball diamond, with the cook "behind the plate." Place a spoonful of filling in the center of each won ton wrapper. Fold the wrapper envelope-style (first and third bases folded in, followed by home plate; then roll the wrapper forward toward second). Seal the final flap with a thin paste made from:

1 tablespoon (15 mL) flour

2 tablespoons (30 mL) cold water

Fry in a skillet in about one inch (2.5 cm) of cooking oil until golden brown.

Let cool, draining on paper towels.

Serve as treats at the Reader's Theater performance.

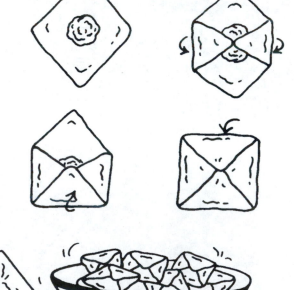

By the Great Hornspoon!
by Sid Fleischman

Summary

The date is January 27, 1849. Jack Flagg, a twelve-year-old orphan, has decided to run away to California and find gold in order to save the family home and support his Aunt Arabella and his sisters, Constance and Sarah. Jack and the elegant butler, Praiseworthy, are forced to stow away on the *Lady Wilma* when their passage money is stolen on the crowded docks of Boston Harbor. Once at sea, Jack and Praiseworthy deal with Captain Swain, the "Wild Bull of the Seas," who is engaged in a race to San Francisco with the *Sea Raven*.

Once in California, our heroes quickly learn the ways of San Francisco and the gold camps. They survive a stage robbery and earn the nicknames "Jamoka Jack" and "Bullwhip." On August 15, 1849, while digging a grave for the villain Cut-Eye Higgins, they strike gold! The story ends with a happy twist as Jack's Aunt Arabella and sisters arrive unexpectedly in San Francisco. Praiseworthy proposes to Aunt Arabella—who accepts—and they all begin to feel like a family.

The outline below is a suggested plan for using the various activities that are presented in this unit. You should adapt these ideas to fit your classroom situation.

Sample Plan

Lesson 1

- Read Chapters 1-3.
- Reading Comprehension (page 35)
- Character Web (page 43)
- Vocabulary/Spelling (page 44)
- Using the Stars (page 58)
- Navigation (page 59)
- Ship's Drill Relays (page 34)
- Step Drawing (page 68)

Lesson 2

- Read Chapters 4-7.
- Reading Comprehension (page 35)
- Vocabulary/Spelling (page 45)
- Travel Poster (page 67)
- Quick Write (page 44)
- Ship's Log (page 44)
- Where in the World activity (page 38)
- Lady Wilma Ship Model (pages 39, 40)

Lesson 3

- Read Chapters 8-11.
- Reading Comprehension (page 36)
- Road Agents and Outlaws activity (pages 54, 55)
- Gold Coins activity (page 69)
- Reading Response Journal (page 45)
- Letter Writing (page 41)

Lesson 4

- Read Chapters 12-15.
- Reading Comprehension (page 36)
- Gold Country Map activity (page 47)
- Similies/Figures of Speech (page 49)
- Design Your Own Coin (page 70)
- Songs of the Gold Rush (page 66)

Lesson 5

- Read Chapters 16-18.
- Reading Comprehension (page 37)
- Paragraph Tag activity (page 46)
- A Weighty Matter (page 64)
- Environmental Studies activity (pages 61-63)
- Culminating Activities—Mining Camp Simulation, A Treasure Chest of Gold (page 72-77)

Overview of Activities

Setting the Stage

1. Introduce the story and concept of life in a mining camp and the effects of "gold fever," by starting your own "gold rush" in the classroom. Conceal small pieces of yellow-gold construction paper around the room (about half as many "nuggets" as you have students). Tell your students that the pieces of paper represent gold, and they have only a short time to locate the treasure. Lay the ground rules for behavior. Contrast your own ground rules with miner's law in the gold camps. Discuss searching (mining) techniques used and the value of partners. Then give the class three to five minutes to search the room.

   When the time is up, check and discuss the mining results with the class. Divide the class into heterogeneous groups of four-student "mining companies" for the next five days. Have each group choose a name and design a logo for the company. Compare this activity to gold fever in California and explain how news of the discovery spread to all parts of the world. On a map or globe, locate the San Francisco Bay area and Boston Harbor. Introduce Jack as the central character of *By the Great Hornspoon!*

2. Construct a bulletin board, using a map of North and South America and the sea routes from Boston to San Francisco as a focal point for reading *By the Great Hornspoon!* (See page 48 for a map to enlarge for classroom use.) Plot the characters' progress toward California as you read.

3. Seeing and touching something that was part of the historical period being studied can be the experience that makes the lesson come alive for your students! "Jackdaws" are actual examples (or reproductions) of primary source material that exhibit for your students what life was like in an earlier time. Jackdaws may be photographs, advertisements, newspapers, posters, or historical documents such as contracts or treaties.

   Jackdaws are a part of most history books as illustrations, and are available in kits such as the "California Gold Rush—1849" kit compiled by Andrew Bronin. Excellent photographs of the period are available in books such as *Children of the Wild West* by Russell Freedman. Your students may have jackdaws in their homes. When introducing this unit, you may want to invite parents to "share and tell" about family keepsakes from the gold rush era.

   Display jackdaws of the period to provide an interesting room environment and set the mood for the California gold rush era.

4. Draw a picture of the *Lady Wilma* leaving Boston Harbor. Have students include the exact date it left. Use the step method on page 68 to complete the drawing.

Overview of Activities *(cont.)*

Enjoying the Book

1. Read the chapters of *By the Great Hornspoon!* as a class, individually, or assign reading to "mining company" cooperative groups.

2. Assign S.Q.R.T. (Super Quiet Reading Time) each day for 15-20 minutes.

3. Do discussion/comprehension questions as a classroom activity or in cooperative groups on a chapter-by-chapter basis.

4. Explore character traits of Praiseworthy, the ever-loyal butler. Make a "character web" for Praiseworthy on page 43. A character web is a writing technique which is used to analyze the traits of a main character. When making a character web, students should justify their selection of character traits with examples from the story. The character name is written in the center circle. The second layer contains the character's traits. The third layer gives examples of events from the story to support the trait.

5. Use spelling/vocabulary lists to make word searches, word races, and team spelling bees.

6. Assign creative writing topics, letters to the characters, paragraph tag, and acrostic poetry to round out your language arts program.

7. Expand your students' knowlege of life in gold rush times with the Road Agents and Outlaws activity on pages 54 and 55. Make a "Wanted" poster for Cut-Eye Higgins.

8. While tracking the *Lady Wilma* on the classroom bulletin board, discuss the concepts of latitude and longitude. Why was it colder as the *Lady Wilma* sailed south?

9. Use classroom maps, an atlas, or a globe to complete the social studies skills activity "Where in the World . . ." to trace the origins of the California mining camp immigrants in the story.

10. Develop an appreciation of the accomplishment of sailing around Cape Horn to California with the Using the Stars and Navigation activities. Learn to recognize some of the major constellations. Make an astrolabe and a compass. Use the astrolabe to plot your own latitude on a world map.

11. Discuss similes and figures of speech found in the story. Then illustrate some selected similies on page 49. Discuss comparisons made in literature and how they are used in descriptions.

12. Use a map of California showing San Francisco, Sacramento, and the locations of the mining camps to follow the movements of Jack and Praiseworthy in the story.

13. Make a model of the *Lady Wilma*. See pages 39 and 40.

14. Explore the world of modern gold money in the activities of Gold Coins and Design Your Own Coin on pages 69 and 70.

Overview of Activities *(cont.)*

Extending the Book

---

1. Every period of history has its special songs. Stephen Foster, America's most famous song writer of the nineteenth century, wrote many of his compositions around the time of the California gold rush. Two of the most famous melodies, "Oh, Susanna" (1848) and "Camptown Races" (1850) provided enjoyment for the miners—especially with an appropriate change of lyrics. Enjoy singing them to the familiar tunes!

   Use Songs of the Gold Rush on page 66 to explore entertainment. Have students write new lyrics for "Oh, Susanna" and perform the song at the Mining Camp Simulation activity.

2. Conduct Ship's Drill Relay Races. Arrange your class into "mining companies" for an "end of watch" race. Line up in teams in a starting line position. Place a bell next to the first student on each team. Students must march, run, or hop to a specified destination, run back, pick up the bell and ring it eight times, and then go back to the end of the line.

3. In Chapter 13, the author describes the crowd of people in the gold camp:

   There were Frenchmen, Sonorians, Chileans, Germans, Missourians, Yankees, Englishmen, and Kanakas from the Sandwich Islands.

   Where in the world did all these people come from?

   Divide the class into "mining companies" (cooperative groups). Ask each group to work together on a world map to find the origins of all these gold seekers. Then trace the probable route they would have used to get to California. Based on the length of time it took the *Lady Wilma* to sail from Boston to San Francisco, estimate how long the journey to California would have been for each of these groups of people. Use the map on page 38 to display your answers.

4. Reenact the experiment that proved the validity of Archimedes' Principle—that weightier materials displace less water than lighter materials. Experience how this is actually related to the identification of pure gold in A Weighty Matter on page 64. Explore the connection to the town of Eureka, California.

5. As a culminating activity, involve your class in a Mining Camp Simulation (pages 72-77).
   * Establish a mining camp and give it a name.
   * Publish mining and camp laws.
   * Select some students to be shopkeepers and city officials.
   * Open restaurants.
   * Set the value of "gold."
   * Make miner's stew, sowbelly and beans, and hardtack to be served at the simulation.
   * Play Claim Jumpers Tag and Ship's Drill Relay Races.

6. Use the final activity, A Treasure Chest of Gold, to extend learning by having individuals or groups ("mining companies") research other gold rushes, gold money of earlier times, characteristics of gold itself, and influences of gold on language and literature. Portions of this page may be used periodically during the unit to enrich learning and enjoyment.

Discussion/Reflection Questions

After reading chapters 1 through 3, engage the students in the following discussion/reflection questions.

Chapters 1-3

1. What do you think a pot-bellied stove is?

2. Why do you think Captain Swain is called the "Wild Bull of the Seas"?

3. Why did Jack and Praiseworthy not buy tickets to California?

4. What do you think "California Fever" was?

5. Why was it so important for Jack and Praiseworthy to go to California?

6. What did the Captain mean when he said Jack was "a lad with stuffings"?

7. As a penalty for being stowaways, the Captain sent Praiseworthy and Jack below to shovel coal. Do you think this was fair punishment? How did it work out for Praiseworthy and Jack?

8. What part did the pig have in Praiseworthy's plan to catch the thief?

9. Why do you think Jack and the pig became friends?

10. Describe daily life aboard the *Lady Wilma*.

11. Captain Swain had to make a difficult decision when the *Sea Raven* came upon the square rigger. What did the Captain do? Would you have done it? Why or why not?

After reading chapters 4-7, engage the students in the following discussion/reflection questions.

Chapters 4-7

1. Cut-Eye Higgins was a real scoundrel. What did he do just before he left the *Lady Wilma?*

2. How did Good Luck finally escape the ship's cook?

3. How did the weather change as the *Lady Wilma* got farther away from Rio de Janeiro?

4. Find Patagonia on a map. What is the nearest continent?

5. Describe the weather as the *Lady Wilma* went around Cape Horn.

6. What were the Fires of Tierra del Fuego? Why did Jack not see them as they rounded Cape Horn?

7. Mr. Azariah Jones and Monsieur Gaunt had big problems. What were they, and how did Praiseworthy help to solve them?

Discussion/Reflection Questions (cont.)

After reading chapters 8-11, engage students in the following discussion/reflection questions.

Chapters 8-11

1. How did Captain Swain win the race between the *Sea Raven* and the *Lady Wilma*?

2. San Francisco was a busy place. Why was there so much activity?

3. Jack and Praiseworthy were faced with a problem almost immediately after arriving in San Francisco. What was the problem, and how did they solve it?

4. Quartz Jackson was concerned about his fiancée arriving from Monterey. Find Monterey on a map. What other towns once served as the capital of California?

5. What do you think Jack thought of the Indians?

6. Describe the passengers on the stagecoach.

7. During the stage coach robbery, we find out that Praiseworthy has a picture of Aunt Arabella. Why do you think he has it?

8. Why did the robbers want the coats? How did this complicate things for Jack and Praiseworthy?

9. Why were there not any women in the mining towns?

10. What happened when Jack and Praiseworthy reached the diggings?

After reading chapters 12-15, engage the students in the following discussion/reflection questions.

Chapters 12-15

1. In chapter 12, the author lets us know that Jack is very fond of Praiseworthy. How does he do this?

2. Jack and Praiseworthy have a conversation about Aunt Arabella. Do you think this could be foreshadowing of future events? Why or why not? Explain.

3. What did Dr. Buckbee offer in his letter? Praiseworthy did not seem interested. Why?

4. Why did the auctioneer say that neckties would fetch a dollar apiece "back in the United States"?

5. Who was Stubb? What happened when Jack and Stubb first met?

6. Do you think Praiseworthy was afraid to fight Mountain Ox? Why?

7. Why did the miner call the Indians "digger Indians"?

8. Who saved Jack from the coyote hole? What was odd about that?

9. Why did Jack and Praiseworthy plan to visit Shirt-tail Camp?

Discussion/Reflection Questions *(cont.)*

After reading chapters 16-18, engage the students in the following Discussion/Reflection Questions.

Chapters 16-18

1. Jack and Praiseworthy went to a lot of trouble to save Cut-Eye Higgins. What did they do? Why?

2. When Jack and Praiseworthy finally saw Dr. Buckbee's map, what did they discover?

3. When Jack and Praiseworthy struck gold, what were they doing? Why?

4. Why was their claim called Gravedigger's Hill?

5. Jonas T. Fletcher called Praiseworthy and Mountain Ox "gladiators." Why did he call them that? What were gladiators?

6. A tragedy was in store for Jack and Praiseworthy on board the riverboat bound for San Francisco. Was there a foreshadowing of these events? If so, what was it?

7. Why did the sailors on the riverboat keep raising the steam pressure in the boiler?

8. How did the Peruvian cats help Jack and Praiseworthy?

9. The story ends with Praiseworthy about to marry Aunt Arabella. Could this have happened if they had lived in Boston? Why?

By the Great Hornspoon!

Where in the World Did All These People Come From?

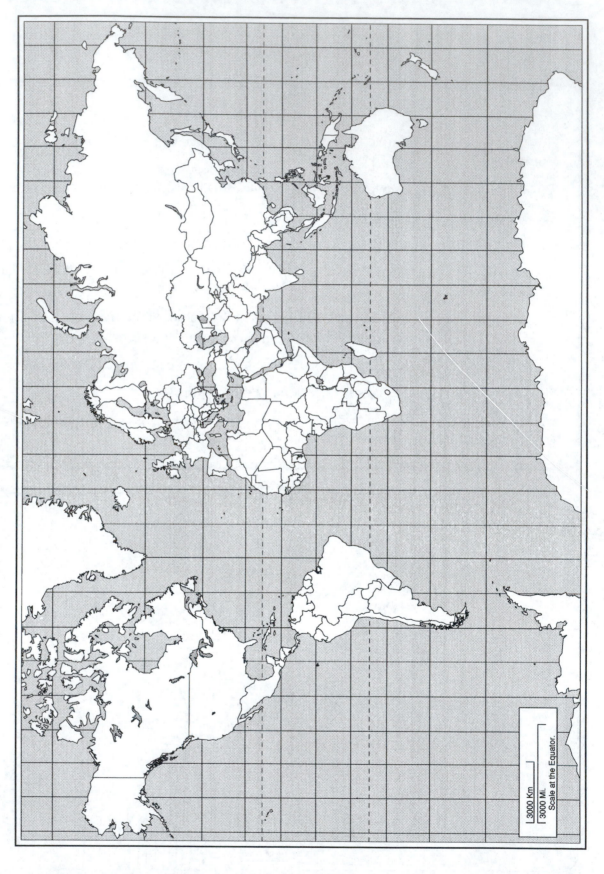

Model of the *Lady Wilma*

The *Lady Wilma* sailed through many miles of ocean. Have "mining companies" make a three-dimensional model of the ocean using the following materials: plaster of Paris, water, straws, plywood or heavy cardboard, poster paints, paintbrushes, pan.

Following the package directions, pour a plaster-of-Paris mixture onto the cardboard or plywood. (**Caution:** Do not pour the mixture into a sink or toilet.) With the straw, blow gently over the surface to form waves; work quickly. After drying, paint the ocean. Make a three-dimensional model of the *Lady Wilma* and place it in the ocean. Add group-created ship's logs and display.

Model of the *Lady Wilma*

fold

1. Cut on outside lines.

2. Fold and glue where indicated.

3. Assemble the hull.

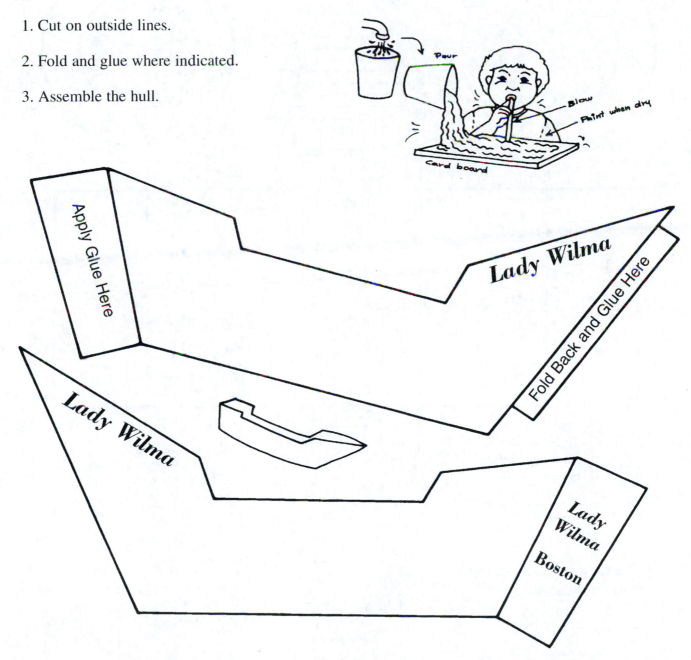

Model of the *Lady Wilma* (cont.)

4. Cut on outside edges, fold, and apply glue where indicated. Assemble deck.

5. Glue bow, stern, and sides of deck. Assemble to the hull.

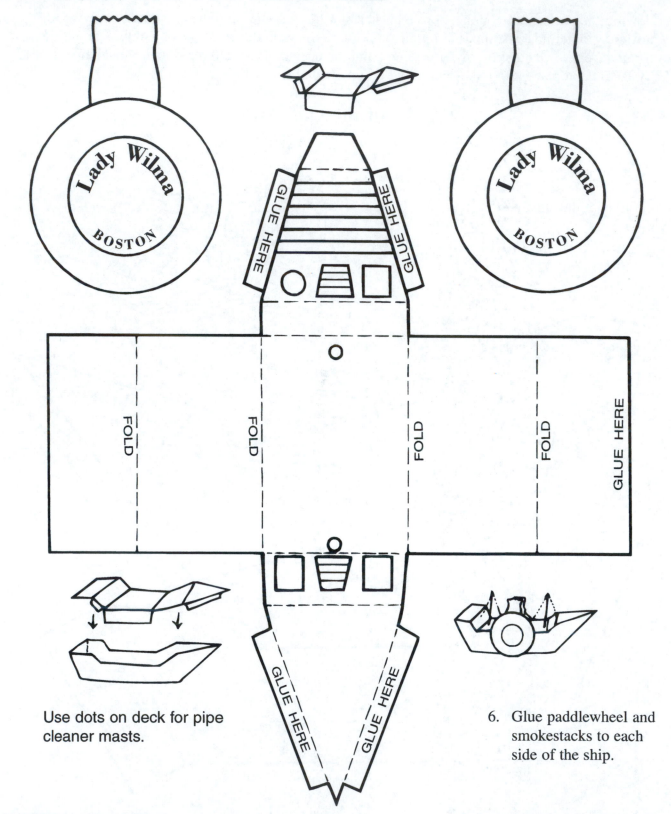

Use dots on deck for pipe cleaner masts.

6. Glue paddlewheel and smokestacks to each side of the ship.

Writing Letters

Letters were the only way that Jack could communicate with Aunt Arabella back in Boston. Jack's letters carried messages that held the characters together across thousands of miles. Before doing the writing assignment on the bottom of the page, review these parts of a friendly letter:

HEADING

The complete address of the writer and the date the letter is written.

SALUTATION

The greeting: "Dear" followed by the name of the person to whom the letter is written.

BODY

The main part of the friendly letter—the message and information you wish to send.

CLOSING

The ending of the letter, followed by the signature of the writer.

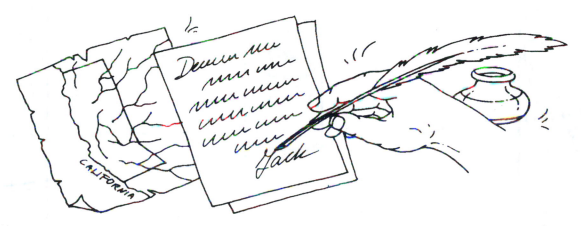

Let's Review . . .

Identify the parts of this letter:

I'm really happy that you are well.   _____

I am fine, and I miss you very much.   _____

Dear Aunt Arabella,   _____

3 Dock Street   _____
San Francisco, California
May 2, 1849

Writing Assignment

Imagine that you are Jack. Write a letter to Aunt Arabella trying to persuade her to come and live in California. Use the stationery on the next page for your letter.

Writing and Word Study

Writing/Ship's Log

The voyage around the Horn was full of adventures for young Jack. Have students choose one and retell it from Captain Swain's point of view. After all members of the "mining company" (cooperative group) have edited their work, put these stories together to make a Ship's Log for the voyage of the *Lady Wilma.*

As a quick-write prompt, ask students to respond to the following question: If you struck it rich, what would you do?

Make each "mining company" (cooperative group) responsible for editing the work of its members. Have each member of the group read another member's paper for five minutes, and then pass the paper to another member until everyone in the group has had the opportunity to help everyone else edit their work.

Vocabulary/Spelling

Divide the class into "mining companies" (cooperative groups). Ask each group to look up the following words and discuss their meanings. Tell each group that they will be working together to design a spelling or vocabulary activity that will be used by the rest of the class. They will write "missing word" sentences in which the "missing words" must be supplied from the vocabulary list. An answer key must be provided by each group.

bowler hat	horizon	jackknife
morsel	monotony	umbrella
skedaddle	bountiful	starboard
immigrant	extraordinary	stalwart
reimburse	enormous	

Writing and Word Study *(cont.)*

Writing/Reading Response Journal

Ask students to begin a response journal for their reading about Jack's adventures in California. Start by describing each day in the mining towns, using appeals to all five senses—seeing, hearing, touching, smelling, tasting.

Vocabulary/Spelling

Group students into "mining companies" for spelling and vocabulary activities. To prepare for the activities, ask each mining company to write each of the vocabulary list words below on a 3" x 5" (7.5 cm x 12.5 cm) card.

fascination	bandana	awesome
buckskin	isthmus	ruffian
stagecoach	nugget	grubstake
poisonous	compassionate	speculation

Hold a Mining Company Word Race. Using the index card words, ask the mining companies to work as quickly as possible to complete the following tasks:

1. Arrange the words in alphabetical order.

2. Arrange the words in the order that they appeared in the chapter.

3. Arrange the words in parts-of-speech categories—nouns, verbs, etc.

4. Use a dictionary to locate the page on which each word is found and write the page number next to the word.

Writing and Word Study *(cont.)*

Paragraph Tag

Divide students into their "mining companies" (cooperative groups) to play Paragraph Tag. Divide the word list on this page equally among the mining companies. Announce that they must tell the first paragraph of a story about the mining camp. Set a timer and have each company write one paragraph only, using each of the words correctly in one sentence.

When the time is up, have each company pass their page to the next company, who will then add a new paragraph (using their words only) to continue the story. When each mining company has written a paragraph on each page, choose a miner from each company to read their version of the story to the class.

Word List for Paragraph Tag

Reproduce this list for each "mining company," or write it on the board, or show it on an overhead projector.

varmint	paunchy	lithe
invincible	brawler	confound
proboscis	undaunted	exuberance
gladiator	provision	conscience
bandana	heinous	

Writing and Word Study

Writing/Ship's Log

The voyage around the Horn was full of adventures for young Jack. Have students choose one and tell it from Captain Swain's point of view. After all members of the "mining company" (cooperative group) have edited their work, put these stories together to make a Ship's Log for the voyage of the *Lady Wilma*.

As a quick-write prompt, ask students to respond to the following question: If you struck it rich, what would you do?

Make each "mining company" (cooperative group) responsible for editing the work of its members. Have each member of the group read another member's paper for five minutes, and then pass the paper to another member until everyone in the group has had the opportunity to help everyone else edit their work.

Vocabulary/Spelling

Divide the class into "mining companies" (cooperative groups). Ask each group to look up the following words and discuss their meanings. Tell each group that they will be working together to design a spelling or vocabulary activity that will be used by the rest of the class. They will write "missing word" sentences in which the "missing words" must be supplied from the vocabulary list. An answer key must be provided by each group.

bowler hat	horizon	jackknife
morsel	monotony	umbrella
skedaddle	bountiful	starboard
immigrant	extraordinary	stalwart
reimburse	enormous	

Writing Letters

Letters were the only way that Jack could communicate with Aunt Arabella back in Boston. Jack's letters carried messages that held the characters together across thousands of miles. Before doing the writing assignment on the bottom of the page, review these parts of a friendly letter:

HEADING

The complete address of the writer and the date the letter is written.

SALUTATION

The greeting: "Dear" followed by the name of the person to whom the letter is written.

BODY

The main part of the friendly letter—the message and information you wish to send.

CLOSING

The ending of the letter, followed by the signature of the writer.

Let's Review . . .

Identify the parts of this letter:

I'm really happy that you are well. _____

I am fine, and I miss you very much. _____

Dear Aunt Arabella, _____

3 Dock Street _____
San Francisco, California
May 2, 1849

Writing Assignment

Imagine that you are Jack. Write a letter to Aunt Arabella trying to persuade her to come and live in California. Use the stationery on the next page for your letter.

Stationery

Praiseworthy's Character W...

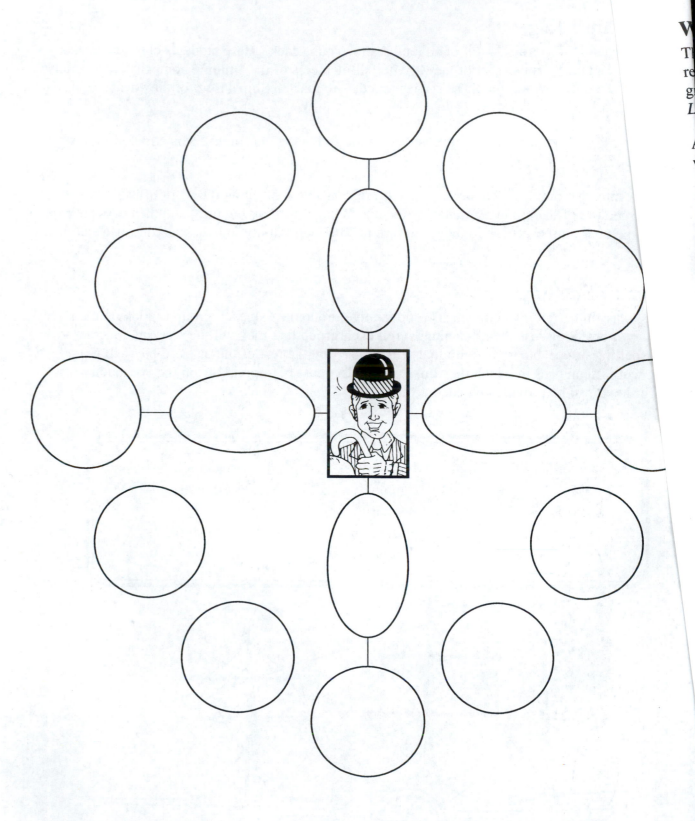

W...

T...
re...
g...
L...

A...
v...

N...
I...

By the Great Hornspoon!

Gold Country Map

Trace the movements of Jack and Praiseworthy from San Francisco through the gold country and back to San Francisco.

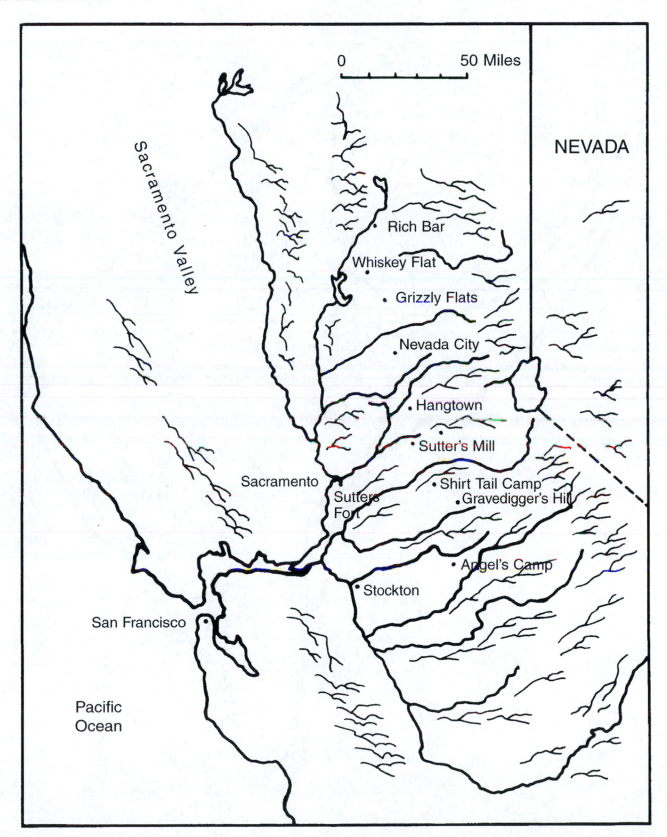

Map of Sea Routes

Similes/Figures of Speech

A *simile* is a figure of speech that uses the words *like* or *as* to compare one object with another unlike object. Here are some similes. Read each one carefully and then write the two unlike things in each sentence that are being compared.

- Praiseworthy was as tall as Quartz Jackson and as straight as an awning post.

- Jack turned as white as a sheet when he saw the bear.

Here are some interesting comparisons taken from *By the Great Hornspoon!* Choose one or find another one you like better from the story and illustrate it below.

- "Wooden awnings stretched over the store fronts like eyeshades."

- "The stagecoach climbed as if it were part mountain goat."

- "The store shacks on both sides of the street were raised on wood pilings like short legs, and looked as if they had just walked into town."

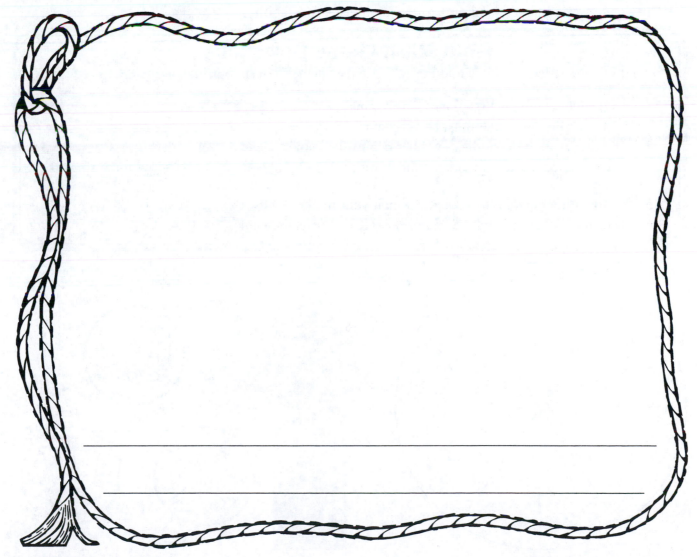

Gold Rush Game

Use the Gold Rush Game to familiarize your students with life in the gold fields. After students have had a chance to play the game in cooperative groups, elicit a class discussion on the dangers and hardships of gold mining. An important discussion question might be "How many people do you think really became rich in the goldfields? Why?"

Game Board

- To make the game board, reproduce the next two pages and connect them at the dotted line.
- Glue the two game board pages to a 12" x 18" (30 cm x 45 cm) piece of construction paper. (Laminating the game board will help it to last longer.)
- The game board can be folded in half and stored easily for later use. Be sure to cut out a set of game directions and glue them to the back of the game board.

Spinner

- Make a spinner for the game by cutting out the arrow and number wheel.
- Glue the number wheel to the tagboard for stability.
- With a sharp pencil, make a hole at the center dots on the arrow and the number wheel.
- Then attach the arrow to the number wheel with a brad.
- Cut out separate markers and glue to tagboard disks for stability.

Gold Rush Game Directions

Pretend you are stricken with "Gold Fever." Use the spinner to test your luck in the GOLD RUSH!

1. To decide who goes first, each player spins.
2. Spins landing on a line must be repeated.
3. The player with the highest number begins the game. Ties go over.
4. Players select separate markers and advance them on the board in accord with the spins they make.
5. Follow directions in the space in which your marker lands.
6. The first player to reach "STRIKE IT RICH!" wins the game.

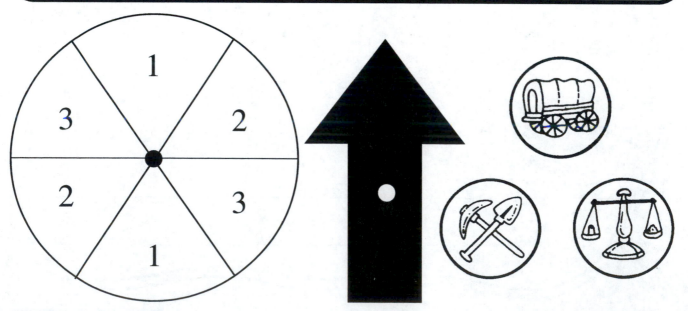

Gold Rush Game *(cont.)*

San Francisco, 1849 **START!** 1	Leave for the gold fields immediately by stagecoach. Advance one space. 2	Stagecoach robbery! You lose everything. Return to San Francisco. 3	Buy mining equipment and supplies in San Francisco. 4

	A great big miner "jumps" your claim. Lose one turn. 15	You become a successful merchant. Take two extra spins! 14	You find a nugget in the stream! Advance two spaces. 13

Use your gold nugget to buy a good meal and clean clothes. Advance one space. 16

You stake a new claim and decide to mine with a "cradle" instead of a pan. Take an extra spin. 17

Jealous of their success, miners pass laws against "foreigners." Lose one turn. 18	A grizzly bear chases you up a tree. You must wait for help. Lose one turn. 19	You find a rich deposit of gold! Advance to "Strike It Rich!" 20

Gold Rush Game *(cont.)*

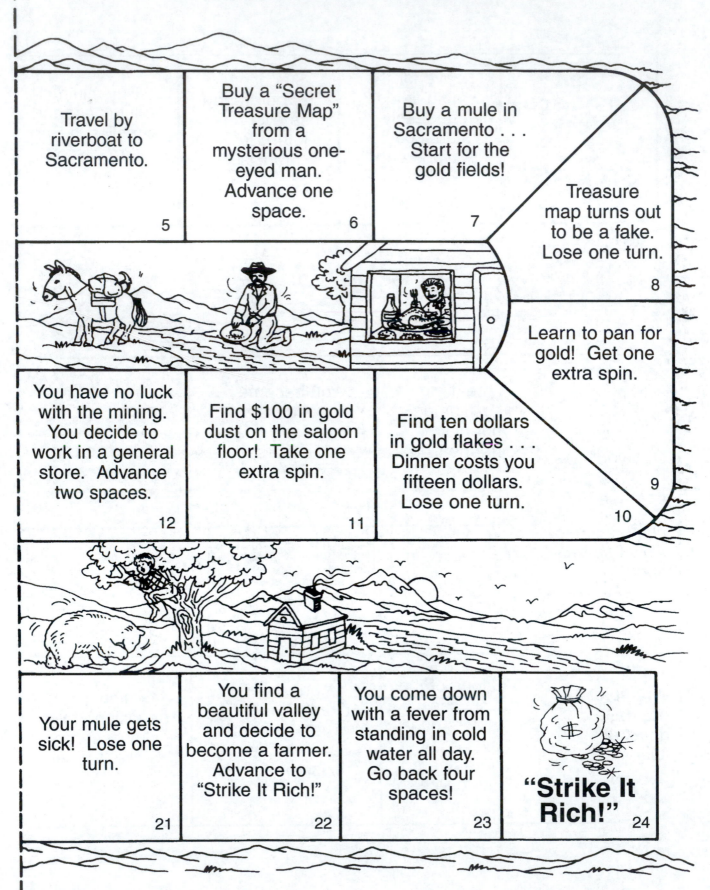

Travel by riverboat to Sacramento.

5

Buy a "Secret Treasure Map" from a mysterious one-eyed man. Advance one space.

6

Buy a mule in Sacramento . . . Start for the gold fields!

7

Treasure map turns out to be a fake. Lose one turn.

8

Learn to pan for gold! Get one extra spin.

You have no luck with the mining. You decide to work in a general store. Advance two spaces.

12

Find $100 in gold dust on the saloon floor! Take one extra spin.

11

Find ten dollars in gold flakes . . . Dinner costs you fifteen dollars. Lose one turn.

10

9

Your mule gets sick! Lose one turn.

21

You find a beautiful valley and decide to become a farmer. Advance to "Strike It Rich!"

22

You come down with a fever from standing in cold water all day. Go back four spaces!

23

"**Strike It Rich!**"

24

Make a Class Gold Rush Book

Make a class Big Book to remember your gold rush activities.

You can purchase blank Big Books at teacher-supply stores or make your own.

Materials:

- Tagboard or cardboard for the cover
- Large sheets of heavy paper for the pages
- Hinged metal rings
- Hole punch

Have students select their favorite two-dimensional (or photograph of three-dimensional) work to be displayed on their very own page in the class book. Make sure students add an explanation of the importance of the piece they have chosen and why they chose it.

Assign special details for completing the book to cooperative groups. Parts to be completed include the following:

Front Cover: Decorate, using title and room number.

Title Page: Include book title, room number, date, and illustration.

Table of Contents: List each work, giving each student's name and page numbers.

Back Cover: (Not to be neglected!) Include illustrations appropriate to the title.

Road Agents and Outlaws: Black Bart

In the early days of California, passengers, mail, and the Wells Fargo strong box were carried throughout the state by stagecoach. The drivers of these stagecoaches were highly skilled at managing their unwieldy vehicles and animals over dangerous, winding mountain roads, often risking death several times a week to bring their stage in on time. The one thing that struck fear in the hearts of this sturdy bunch was the possibility of being "held up" by the legendary Black Bart.

Black Bart held up 28 stagecoaches in Northern California. His trademarks were always the same. He wore a long linen duster, a flour sack over his head with two holes cut out for eyes, and always said the words, "Throw down the box!"

Black Bart came to be known as the "Gentleman Bandit" because although he pointed a shotgun at the stagecoach drivers during robberies, he never fired it. He never took anything from stagecoach passengers, and he usually left a poem behind, which he signed "Black Bart, the PO-8."

Black Bart was finally caught in 1883. He turned out to be a respected mining engineer named Charles E. Bolton. He served five years in San Quentin prison for his crimes.

Here I lay me down to sleep
To wait the coming morrow,
Perhaps success, perhaps defeat,
And everlasting sorrow.
Let come what will, I'll try it on,
My condition can't be worse;
And if there's money in that box,
"'Tis munny in my purse!"
Respectfully,
Black Bart, the PO-8

Discussion Questions

1. Why was Black Bart feared by stagecoach drivers?

2. Why was Black Bart called the "Gentleman Bandit"?

3. When was Black Bart finally caught?

4. Who was Black Bart?

5. Why do you think he robbed stagecoaches?

Wanted Poster

Complete the following "Wanted" poster for Cut-Eye Higgins.

WANTED

"Cut-Eye" Higgins

Also Known As

_____

For the Crimes of

_____

A Reward of _____ Dollars Has Been Offered

by

_____

for This Brigand's Capture.

Gold Rush Math

Forty-Niners worked hard to pan their gold out of California streams, and they needed sharp math skills to exchange their gold correctly for the things they needed.

Keep your math skills as sharp as a Forty-Niner's.

Solve these puzzles:

Add the numbers in each row and column and along each diagonal. Also, add the numbers in each of the four corners. Each of the sums must equal 34.

		3	
5			
			12
	14		

7			14
		10	
			13
9			

Complete each of these grids so that there are subtraction facts across and down.

8	–	4	=	
–	Gold	–	⛏	–
5	–	2	=	
=	⛏	=	Fever	=
		–		=

14	–	5	=	
–	Cali-fornia	–	🛒	–
7	–	3	=	
=	⚖	=	or Bust!	=
		–		=

Gold in California!

During the gold rush in California, an ounce of gold was worth sixteen dollars. The gold itself, in the form of flakes, dust, or nuggets, was used by the miners in place of paper currency to buy the goods and services they needed.

Use the conversion chart below to figure out how much gold you would need to buy the things a Forty-Niner would need in the mining camps.

Weight/Mass

1 pound (lb) = 16 ounces (oz)   1 dram (dr) = 27.343 grains (gr)

1 ounce (oz) = 16 drams, or 437.5 grains (gr)   1 grain (gr) = 0.0036 drams (dr)

Which of these would you need to buy? Choose carefully, and then calculate the amount of gold necessary for each purchase. How long do you think it would take you to mine the amount of gold needed? Check your answers with other members of your class.

Flour...$1.00 a pound _____

Bear Steak...$2.00 _____

Candles...$1.00 each _____

Sowbelly and Beans...$1.00 a bowl _____

Eggs...$1.00 each _____

Boots...$20.00 _____

Salt Pork...50 cents a pound _____

Hot Tub Bath...$10.00 _____

Picks and Shovels...$20.00 each _____

Hammer...$10.00 _____

Nails...50 cents each _____

Saleratus (baking soda)...$1.50 _____

Bread...$1.00 a slice _____

with butter...$2.00 _____

Hay...8 cents a pound _____

Rifle...$35.00 _____

Onions...$1.50 a pound _____

Blanket...$50.00 _____

A Night in a "Hotel"...$20.00 _____

Riverboat fare from Sacramento City to San Francisco...$25.00 _____

Using the Stars

Many people in the East who read about the discovery of gold in California were stricken with gold fever and chose the quickest route to the gold fields, which was by sea. The ships' captains used the stars to find their way. How well do you know the stars above you? Read and learn about these star clusters. Try to find them in the night sky.

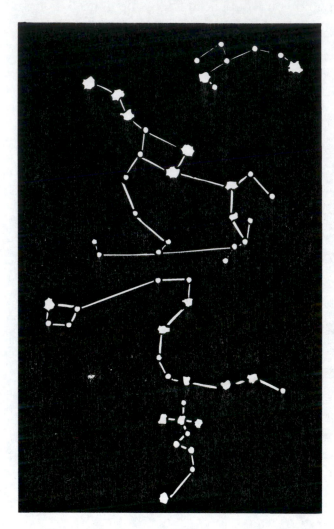

Little Dipper or Ursa Minor

The first star in the handle of the Little Dipper is the North Star. This star always points north. The Little Dipper can be seen in the northern sky all year long.

Big Dipper or Ursa Major

Use the Big Dipper to help find the North Star. Imagine a line through the two outside stars of the cup. Keep looking up until the North Star is visible.

Draco or The Dragon

According to Greek legend, Ladon the sleeping dragon was told to guard Hera's apple tree. One day Heracles tricked Ladon and sliced off his head. To punish Ladon, Hera changed him into a constellation of stars—Draco, the Dragon.

Casseopeia or The Queen

Casseopeia was a boastful queen who often bragged about her own and her daughter's beauty. The gods punished her by making her appear upside down. Thus, depending on the season, Casseopeia looks like a W or an M.

On-Your-Own Projects

The ancient Greeks used mythology to explain the various constellations. Research and write a report about how one of the constellations got its name. An excellent resource book for this project is *The Stargazer's Guide to the Galaxy* by Q. L. Pierce (RGA Publishing Group, 1991).

- Find out your astrological sign. Draw a picture of your sign's constellation.

- Read and learn the definition of "star."

- Draw the stars in the constellation of your choice. Then draw the figure it represents. For example, if you have chosen Casseopeia, draw the W arrangement of stars and then the Queen.

- Find out what "Ursa" in Ursa Major and Ursa Minor refers to. Report your information to the class.

Navigation

Ships' captains navigated by one star in the northern hemisphere and another when they sailed south of the equator. In the northern hemisphere, it was Polaris—the North Star—that helped sailors find their way. You can find Polaris in the night sky by locating the Little Dipper. Polaris is the last star in the "handle" of the Little Dipper.

The Astrolabe

You can make an astrolabe—a real tool—to use the stars to navigate. Start with an 8" (20 cm) diameter tagboard semicircle. Create a protractor by marking the degrees from the 0 degree center of the curved edge to the 90 degree straight edge. Tie a 6" (15 cm) piece of string around the center of a drinking straw. Then tie a large paper clip 4" (10 cm) from the straw. Glue the straw to the straight edge of the tagboard.

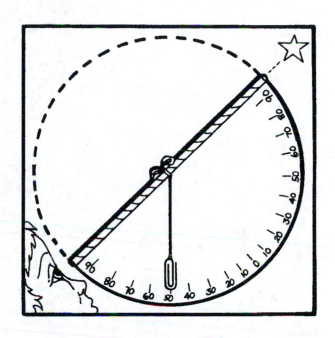

To find your location in latitude anywhere on earth, just take your astrolabe outside on a clear night. Hold your astrolabe with the straight side up, and then sight Polaris through the straw. Press the paper clip carefully against the tagboard with your finger and read your location in degrees of latitude. Find your position in latitude on the map on page 60.

The Compass

The compass is also an important navigational tool. Make your own compass-in-a-dish like this. For each compass, you will need the following materials:

- one large sewing needle
- a piece of cork or foam packing material
- a saucer
- water
- a magnet

Partially fill the saucer with water. Slide one end of the magnet along the length of the needle, stroking in the same direction 20 times. (This process will magnetize the needle.) Place the newly magnetized needle on the cork and float it on the water in the saucer. Watch as the needle settles into a north-south pattern.

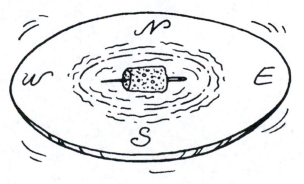

Navigation *(cont.)*

World Map

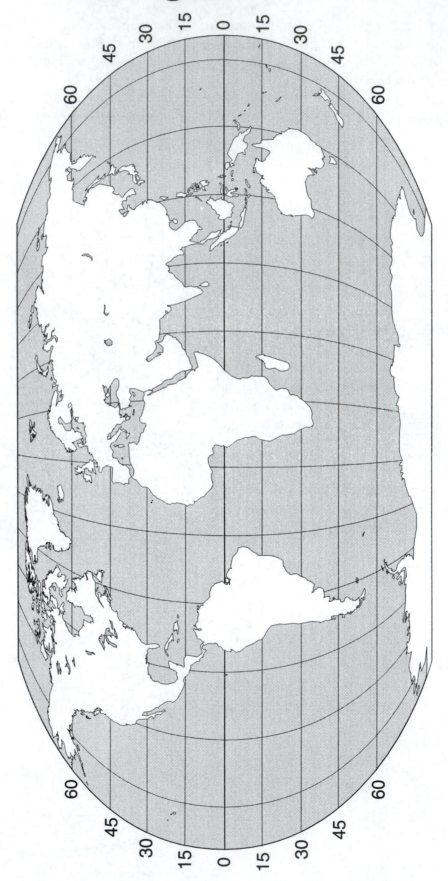

Environmental Studies

Divide the class into "mining companies" (cooperative groups). Discuss mining techniques with the students. Provide library resources and illustrations for the following mining techniques: panning, windlass and shaft mining, hydraulic mining, the cradle, and the long tom.

Panning

The most widely-used method of mining in the California gold fields was panning. Miners would put mud and dirt in a pan, lower the pan into a river or stream, and swish the mud around the pan. The heavier gold settled to the bottom while the mud washed away. A miner would often stand for hours in the icy-cold water to find only a few specks of gold.

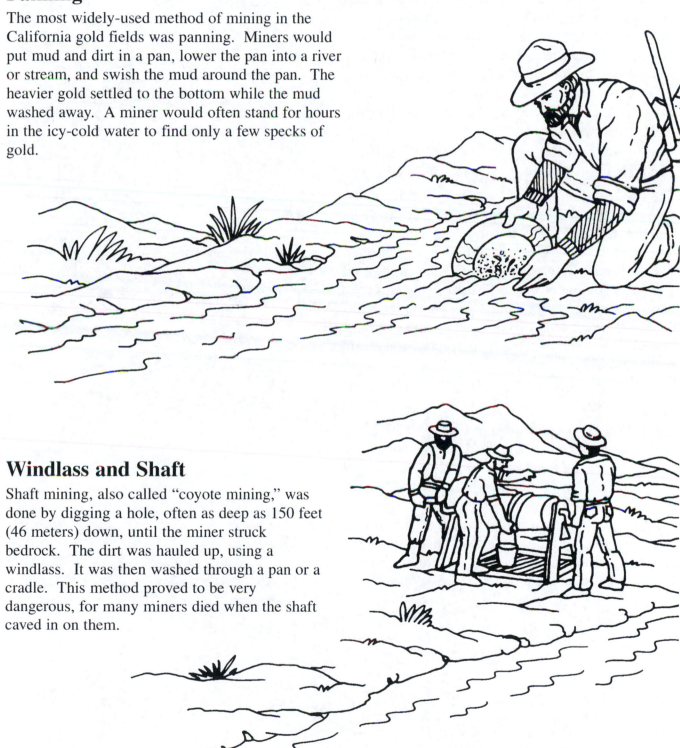

Windlass and Shaft

Shaft mining, also called "coyote mining," was done by digging a hole, often as deep as 150 feet (46 meters) down, until the miner struck bedrock. The dirt was hauled up, using a windlass. It was then washed through a pan or a cradle. This method proved to be very dangerous, for many miners died when the shaft caved in on them.

Environmental Studies *(cont.)*

Hydraulic Mining

Hydraulic mining used high-powered hoses to direct streams of water against the sides of mountains. Tons of water were used to create rivers of mud that were diverted into "long toms," where the gold was collected. Hydraulic mining required a lot of expensive equipment, so only a few large companies could afford to do it. It was the most profitable way to mine, but also the most damaging to the environment. Hydraulic mining was made illegal in most states by 1900.

Cradle

The cradle (which looked like a baby's cradle) took the panning process one step farther. The cradle had a perforated steel top. Mud and dirt were shoveled onto the top, water was poured over it, and the cradle was "rocked." The rocking action allowed the mud and water to run out while the heavy gold was lodged between wooden strips, called "riffles," at the bottom of the cradle. It took two or three men to operate a cradle—one to dig, another to carry dirt, and one to rock the cradle.

Long Tom

The long tom was a wooden trough 10 to 30 feet (3-10 meters) long, with two sides and a bottom. Miners built long toms near rivers and streams so that water could be diverted through them. The bottom of the long tom was constructed with a plate (similar to a cradle), and below that plate were wooden riffles to catch the gold. Using a long tom, miners could get four to five times as much gold as a cradle would produce, but it took many more men to operate it.

Environmental Studies *(cont.)*

Excavating Claims

1. Starting with a bag of soft chocolate chip or oatmeal chocolate chip cookies, explain to the students that each cookie will represent an individual mining claim.

2. Distribute the cookies to the students along with two toothpicks. The toothpicks, of course, represent the mining tools to be used.

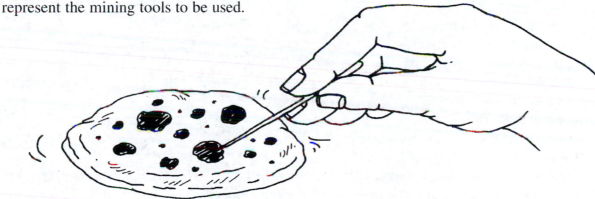

3. Have the students use the mining tools provided to search their claims (the cookies) for gold (the chocolate chips).

4. Remind students to be careful of the environment around their claims.

5. After "mining" for five minutes, ask students to share their experiences.

Questions

1. What happened to the "claims" during the mining process?

2. What might have happened if other mining techniques had been used (hydraulic, for instance)?

3. If mining is absolutely necessary, what can be done to protect the environment?

Activity: Ask each "Mining Company" to make a poster that would persuade miners to protect the environment.

A Weighty Matter

Gold! Down through the ages it has been rare and costly. Few have been able to afford much of the precious metal, so it always surprises us to find out just how heavy pure gold really is.

Long ago, legend tells us the great Greek physicist and mathemetician Archimedes (287?-212 B.C.) once performed a great service for King Hiero of Syracuse. The king had given his goldsmith a great lump of solid gold, instructing him to make a crown. The goldsmith soon returned with a beautifully crafted golden crown. It weighed exactly the same as the original lump of solid gold. Still, King Hiero suspected the goldsmith had kept back some of the gold for himself, mixing some less costly silver into the crown to make up for the lost weight. The king asked Archimedes to find out if the goldsmith had cheated him. It was a tough problem, for one cannot tell by looking if such a thing has been done. Archimedes was stumped.

One day while taking a bath, Archimedes filled the tub too full, and when he stepped in, of course, the water spilled out onto the floor. He suddenly realized that the amount of water moved out of the tub would be EXACTLY the same size (or volume) as the space taken up by his body. He saw the solution to the king's problem, and he was so excited he ran out into the street, shouting "Eureka!" (I have found it!) No doubt the people on the street wondered what in the world he had found, since the famous thinker had forgotten to put any clothes on! Archimedes then compared the amount of water the crown displaced with the amount displaced by an equal weight of pure gold. The crown displaced more water. That meant the crown was not pure gold, but made partly of some lighter metal. The goldsmith had cheated the king! Ever since that time, we have called this idea (that heavier materials do not take up as much space as lighter materials) Archimedes' Principle.

Challenge:

1. Test Archimedes' Principle yourself. You will need one six-ounce (168 g) fishing sinker, six ounces (168 g) of modeling clay, two large, clear plastic measuring cups half-filled with water, and some gold spray-paint. Using all your modeling clay, shape a small kingly crown. Paint it gold along with the fishing sinker. Place each into separate measuring cups. Notice which one—the golden lump or the golden crown, each weighing exactly the same—displaces more water.

2. Locate the town of Eureka on a California map.

3. Why is it appropriate for a town in California to be named Eureka?

Landforms

California has just about every kind of landform that exists in nature. Miners who came to California during the Gold Rush had to cross wide oceans or vast plains, deserts, and high mountains just to get to the gold fields. Once they completed their journey, the miners had to deal with wide rivers, swiftly flowing streams, and steep valleys, not to mention the Sierra Nevada.

Learn the definition for each of the following landforms.

River: A large moving body of water which flows into another body of water, such as a lake, ocean, or another river.

Prairie: A large area of flat or hilly land, covered mostly by grasses.

Desert: A dry, sandy area with little vegetation, getting very little rain.

Mountain: Land that has steep sides and rounded or pointed peaks standing much higher than the land around it.

Ocean: A large body of salt water. Oceans cover most of the earth's surface. The Pacific is the largest of the earth's three oceans.

Landforms Activity

Make a salt-and-flour relief map of California. Start by drawing an outline map of California on a 12" x 18" (30 cm x 45 cm) piece of tagboard or cardboard. Check an atlas for a relief map that will show landform details, and then mold the landforms on your map, using salt-and-flour clay.

Salt-and-Flour Clay

1. Mix equal amounts of salt and flour in a large bowl.

2. Add water a little at a time and stir until the mixture has the consistency of modeling clay.

3. When the landforms are dry, paint the map with tempera paint as follows.

   Blue: rivers, lakes, and oceans
   Green: valleys
   Yellow: desert
   Brown: mountains
   White: mountain peaks

Songs of the Gold Rush

"Oh, Californy!" *(to the tune of 'Oh, Susanna!')*

I come from dear old Boston with a washbowl* on my knee,
I'm going to California, the gold dust for to see.
It rained all night the day I left, the weather it was dry,
The sun so hot I froze to death, dear brother, don't you cry.

> *(CHORUS)*
> *Oh, Cal-i-for-ny!*
> *Oh, that's the land for me!*
> *I'm going to Sacramento*
> *With a washbowl on my knee.*

I jumped aboard the largest ship and traveled on the sea,
And every time I thought of home, I wished it wasn't me!
The vessel reared like any horse that had of oats a wealth,
I found it wouldn't throw me, so I thought I'd throw myself!
(CHORUS)

I thought of all the pleasant times we've had together here,
And I thought I ought to cry a bit, but I couldn't find a tear,
The pilot's bread was in my mouth, the gold dust in my eye,
and I thought I'm going far away, dear brother don't you cry.
(CHORUS)

I soon shall be in Frisco, and there I'll look around,
And when I see the gold lumps there, I'll pick them off the ground.
I'll scrape the mountains clean, my boys, I'll drain the rivers dry,
A pocketful of rocks bring home, so brother, don't you cry.
*A washbowl—the pan miners used to separate gold from sand.

"Around Cape Horn" *(to the tune of 'Camptown Races')*

A bully ship and a bully crew
Dooda, dooda,
A bully mate and a captain too,
O, Dooda, dooda, day.

> *(CHORUS)*
> *Then blow ye winds hi-oh*
> *For Cal-i-for-ny-o,*
> *There's plenty of gold so I've been told*
> *On the banks of the Sacramento.*

Oh, around Cape Horn we're bound to go,
Dooda, dooda,
Around Cape Horn through the sleet and snow,
O, Dooda, dooda, day.
(CHORUS)

Oh, around Cape Horn in the month of May
Dooda, dooda,
Oh, around Cape Horn is a very long way,
O, Dooda, dooda, day.
(CHORUS)

Ninety days to Frisco Bay,
Dooda, dooda,
Ninety days is darn good pay,
O, Dooda, dooda, day.
(CHORUS)

I wish to God I'd never been born,
Dooda, dooda,
To go a-sailin' round Cape Horn
O, Dooda, dooda, day.
(CHORUS)

To the Sacramento we're bound away
Dooda, dooda,
To the Sacramento's a heck of a way,
O, Dooda, dooda, day.
(CHORUS)

California Travel Poster

Pretend you are a gold seeker and the year is 1849. Design and make a travel poster that would make you want to come to California.

The *Lady Wilma*

Draw the *Lady Wilma* leaving port. Use the four-step drawing technique illustrated below. Be sure to include the exact date the *Lady Wilma* left Boston Harbor.

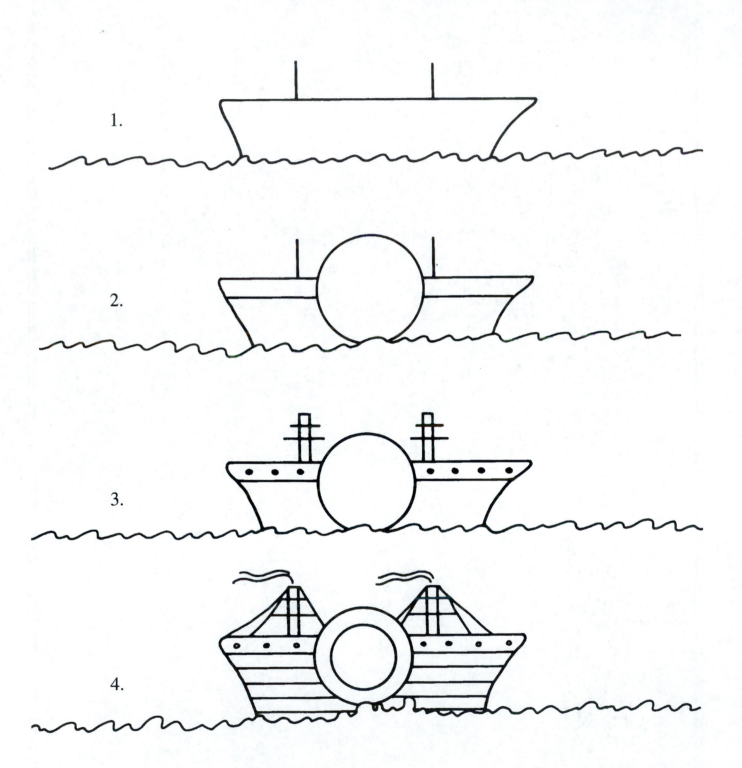

Gold Coins

From ancient times through modern times, humans have valued gold. One of its earliest uses was as money in the form of coins. Prized by collectors for their artistry and high value, gold coins are still being minted today. Among the world's best-known modern gold coins are the following:

- The Eagle
- The Fifty-Peso
- The Krugerrand
- The Panda
- The Maple Leaf
- The Sovereign

Have each "mining company" (cooperative group) research one of the gold coins listed above. They should find answers to the following questions and share their results with the class as a whole.

1. Where is this coin minted? _____

2. When was this coin first minted? _____

3. How much does this coin weigh? _____

4. About how much is this coin worth today? _____

5. What is this coin's approximate size? _____

6. Where can one buy this coin? _____

7. Can you provide a sketch and description of this coin's main design?

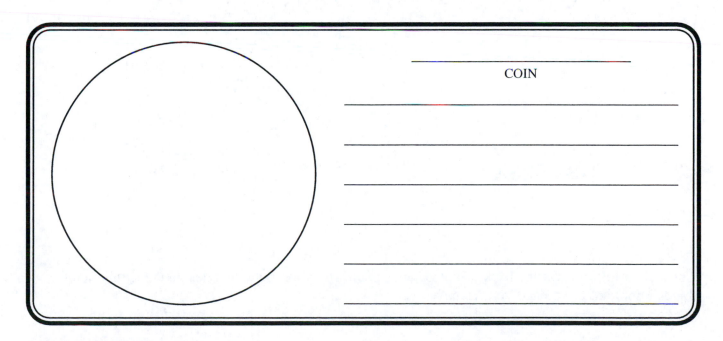

COIN

Design Your Own Coin

Coins are often prized not just because of their precious metal like gold or silver but also because of their artistry of design. Many such coins achieve high fame, like those created by the famous American sculptor, Augustus Saint Gaudens (1848-1907).

Coin designs often show persons, places, and animals that are important in the history of a given country. Also, mottoes are frequently chosen to express an idea important to the people of that country. Before beginning this activity, look carefully at the pictures and words of a coin of your country.

Now, here is your chance to design your own coin. Be sure to include these elements in your original design:

- Name and/or amount of your coin

- Year the coin is minted

- Motto—a brief word or phrase important to you or your country

- Obverse—the side bearing the main design

- Reverse—The side opposite the main design

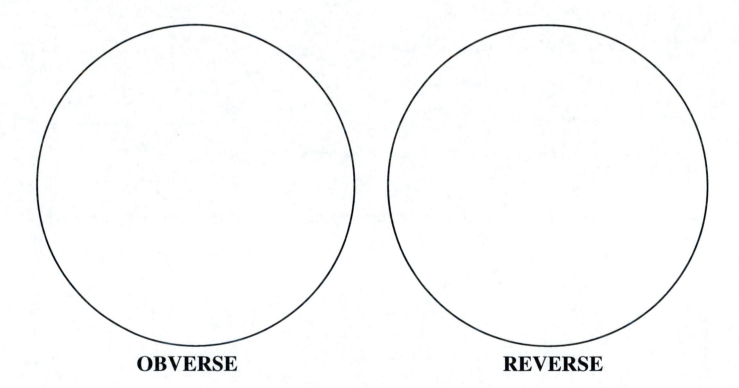

OBVERSE   **REVERSE**

Critical Thinking: On the back of this page, explain why your motto and design are symbolic of things important to you and your country.

How to Pan for Gold

You can learn to pan for gold just like the Forty-Niners did! It is not quite so easy to find gold today as it was during the California gold rush, but there is still plenty to be found. Your chances of finding gold are better if you live in an area where gold has already been found, a gold region. There are many gold regions in the United States. Check the U.S. Gold Map below.

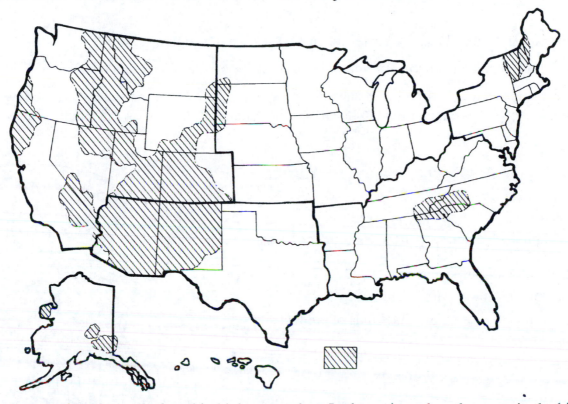

Gold is a heavy mineral usually found in high mountains. In the spring when the snow in the high country melts, there is a "spring runoff." All of this melting snow rushing down the mountains washes gold down into streams and rivers. The gold, being heavier than either sand or rocks, is carried by the running water until the current slows down. Then it drops to the bottom of the stream or river. Be sure to look for gold along the edges of streams where the current is slow.

You will need a heavy, shallow pan (like a pie pan but larger), a shovel, some tweezers, and a small container to put your gold in.

First, use the shovel to dig up some of the mud from the stream bed and put it in your mining pan.

Next, put the pan in the water and move it gently in a flat circular motion until all the dirt is washed away. Only gravel and sand should remain in the pan.

Then, lower the pan into the water again and use the same flat circular motion, rocking the pan from side to side to wash the gravel over the sides of the pan. Gold is heavier than the gravel and should stay in the bottom of the pan. Use the tweezers to look through the remaining sand for shining pieces of gold. The pieces of gold may be as large as a pea or as small as a tiny fleck.

Remember, gold is very soft. You will be able to flatten a piece of gold with your tweezers. Fool's gold (pyrite) looks just like gold, but it is hard and cannot be flattened.

Mining Camp Simulation

Preparation: Paint several dozen pebbles gold, to be used as "nuggets." Hide the "nuggets" in a predetermined "mining area" on the playground, in or near a sandbox. Make cornbread, miner's stew, and sowbelly and beans ahead of time. (See recipes on page 75.) Groups could do the cooking at school, or the cooking may be done at home. Foods should be ready to enjoy as part of the simulation activities.

- Have on hand several balance scales for students to use in weighing "gold."

- As a class, decide on a name for your mining camp before the simulation begins.

- Divide students into "mining companies" and explain their roles in the simulation. Allow these cooperative groups enough time to divide up tasks and take on roles for the simulation activities.

Activities

Newspaper

Design and produce a newspaper for your mining camp.

What will your newspaper be called?

What kind of news articles will it have?

Who will advertise? For what kinds of products and services?

Mining Camp Simulation *(cont.)*

Activities *(cont.)*

City Officials

Elect a town sheriff, deputies, mayor, city councilmen, and a judge.

The mayor and city councilmen will decide on laws for the mining camp, procedures for staking claims, as well as punishments for wrongdoing.

A miners' court will be chosen from the townspeople.

The judge should be prepared to settle any disputes that arise during the simulation.

Restaurant Owners/Operators

Choose a name for the restaurant. Design and make menus for the restaurant.

Decide on an acceptable exchange rate of "gold" for each food item on the menu.

At lunch time "sell" the miners and townspeople miner's stew, sowbelly and beans, and hardtack (along with other appropriate items that entrepreneurial young restaurant operators may have in mind).

Restaurant owners should be prepared to weigh "gold" in exchange for food.

Storekeepers

Storekeepers will decide on the supplies to be sold in the mining camp and set the prices for the supplies in "gold."

In the absence of real goods, coupons to represent mining pans, shovels, wheelbarrows, etc., may be sold to miners.

Storekeepers should be prepared to weigh "gold" in exchange for goods.

Entertainment—Mining Camp Theater

Stage a short play or skit to be presented to the miners and townspeople following lunch.

Use songs and dances from "Wee Sing America" as a good resource.

Set a price for admission (in "gold," of course) and be prepared to weigh "gold" in exchange for the price of admission.

Miners

Look for "gold" in the predetermined mining area on the playground. Take any disputes over claims or mining to the assigned judge and the miners' court.

Keep a log of the number of "gold" nuggets found and the supplies and goods purchased.

Closure/Discussion Questions

1. How was each role in the simulation important?

2. Did the miners ever manage to get rich? Why? Why not?

3. How did the gold rush change California?

Mining Camp Simulation (cont.)

Mining Camp News

Editor:

Claims Jumped!

Story by:

Who:

What:

Where:

When:

Why:

Picture by:

FOR SALE AT THE MINER'S STORE:

Always Bargain Prices!

BIG SHOW TONIGHT AT THE THEATER!

Story by:

DON'T BE LATE!

Mining Camp Simulation *(cont.)*

MINING CAMP RECIPES

Cornbread

1. Combine: 1 cup (250 mL) cornmeal, 1 cup (250 mL) flour, ¼ cup (60 mL) sugar, 1 tablespoon (15mL) baking powder, and 1 teaspoon (5mL) salt.

2. Mix well in a large bowl.

3. Add ⅓ cup (80 mL) cooking oil, 1 egg, and 1 cup (250 mL) milk.

4. Pour into a well buttered 8" (20 cm) square pan.

5. Bake at 400°F (204°C) for 25 minutes.

Miner's Stew

1. Wash carrots, celery, potatoes, green pepper, and onions.

2. Cut vegetables into small pieces and place in a large pot.

3. Add 6-8 cups (2 L) water, 2 cups (.5 L) tomato juice, small amount of diced beef (optional) 6 teaspoons (30 mL) bouillon, and ½ cup (125 mL) butter.

4. Simmer all morning until vegetables (and beef, if added) are tender. Season with salt and pepper and enjoy with cornbread and butter.

Sowbelly and Beans

1. Wash and sort a large package of dry, white navy beans. Be sure to remove any stones or imperfect beans.

2. Soak beans overnight in a large pot of cold water.

3. Add a square of salt pork to the beans, along with some chopped celery and brown onion.

4. Cook over low heat all morning until beans are tender.

5. Remove salt pork square, cut into small pieces, and stir into beans.

6. Season with salt and pepper.

Mining Camp Simulation *(cont.)*

Coupons

(Color, cut out, and use for merchandise at the mining camp store.)

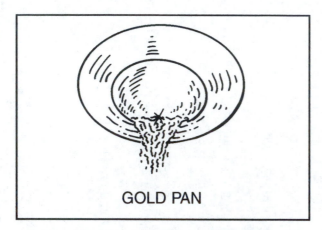

GOLD PAN

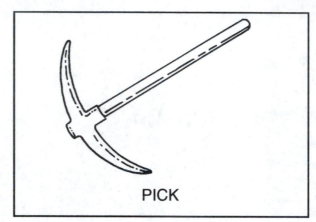

PICK

LONG TOM

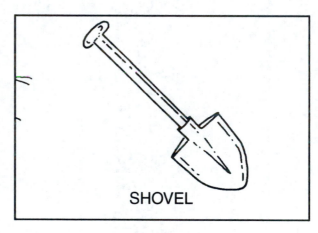

SHOVEL

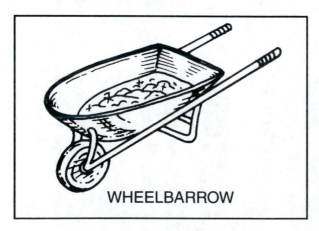

WHEELBARROW

CRADLE

Mining Camp Simulation *(cont.)*

Miner's Log

Miner's Name (and Nickname) _____

Mining Company Name_____ Date _____

Mining Income

Number of Nuggets found	_____
Total Weight	_____
Exchange Rate	$ _____
Total Value	$ _____

Mining Expenses

Items Purchased	Price for Each	Total Cost
SUPPLIES		
Gold Pan		
Cradle		
Long Tom		
Shovel		
Pick		
Wheelbarrow		
FOOD		
Sowbelly & Beans		
Miner's Stew		
Cornbread		
ENTERTAINMENT		
Miner's Theater Admission		
Newspaper		
TOTAL		

Total income $_____ minus total expenses $_____ equals total profit $_____.

Events of the Day

(claims staked, claims jumped, miners' court, etc.)

_____

_____

_____

A Treasure Chest of Gold

Ten Facts of Gold

1. Gold is twice as heavy as lead.
2. One ounce of gold can be drawn into a fine golden wire 50 miles long.
3. One ounce of gold can be hammered into a sheet covering 100 square feet.
4. Corrosion and acids that spoil other metals cannot harm gold. Golden treasure found on ships thousands of years ago is still as good as ever.
5. A glass full of gold is 19 times as heavy as the same glass of water.
6. The deepest gold mine is in South Africa, dropping over two and one-fourth miles into the earth.
7. The largest nugget, "Welcome, Stranger," was found in Australia and weighs 2,217 troy ounces (69 kg).
8. Gold cups and jewelry from as early as 3500 B.C. have been found in Mesopotamia and Egypt.
9. All seawater contains gold in solution.
10. The richest gold field in the world is the Witwatersrand in the Transvaal Province of South Africa.

Ten Stories and Legends of Gold

1. "King Midas and the Golden Touch" (Greece)
2. "The Legend of El Dorado" (Spain)
3. "The Devil's Three Gold Hairs" (Germany)
4. "The Treasure" (Russia)
5. "Jason and the Golden Fleece" (Greece)
6. "The Gold Bug" (United States)
7. "The Goose That Laid the Golden Eggs" (Greece)
8. "The Golden Goose" (Germany)
9. "Boots and the Troll" (Norway)
10. "The Golden Apples of the Hesperides" (Greece—Labors of Hercules)

Ten Famous Gold Rushes

1. Brazil, 1695, 1980
2. Georgia, 1828
3. Australia, 1857
4. New Zealand, 1861
5. British Columbia, 1858
6. Black Hills, Dakota, 1876
7. Klondike, Yukon Territory, 1897
8. Colorado, 1859, 1891
9. South Africa, 1886
10. Alaska, 1899

Ten Old Gold Coins

1. Ducats
2. Florins
3. Doubloons
4. Escudos
5. Bezants
6. Guineas
7. Persian Darius the Great
8. Lydian Lion and Bull
9. Shekels
10. Staters

Ten California Gold Camps

1. Shinbone Creek
2. Angels Camp
3. Humbug Hill
4. Sixbit Gulch
5. Rough and Ready
6. Tin Cup Diggings
7. Cutthroat Bar
8. Whiskey Flat
9. Fiddletown
10. Greenhorn Bar

Ten Terms and Phrases of Gold

1. Silence Is Golden
2. As Good as Gold
3. The Golden Rule
4. The Golden Mean
5. Gild the Lily
6. All That Glitters Is Not Gold
7. A Heart of Gold
8. The Golden Horde
9. Black Gold
10. Gold Is Where You Find It

Bibliography

Ada, Alma F. *The Gold Coin.* MacMillan Child Grp, 1991.

Andrist, Ralph. *The California Gold Rush.* American Heritage Publishing, 1961.

Applegate, Jill, ed. *Gold! Gold! A Beginners Handbook and Recreational Guide: How and Where to Prospect for Gold.* Sierra Trading, 1992.

Bauer, Helen. *California Gold Days.* Doubleday, 1951.

Bloch, Louis M. Jr., ed. *Overland to California in 1859: A Guide for Wagon Train Travelers.* Bloch and Company, 1990.

Blumberg, Rhoda. *The Great American Gold Rush.* Bradbury Press, 1989.

Chambers, Catherine E. *California Gold Rush: Search for Treasure.* Troll Assocs., 1981.

Cole, Joanna, ed. *Best Loved Folk-Tales of the World.* Doubleday, 1982.

Freedman, Russell. *Children of the Wild West.* Clarion Books, 1983.

Gemming, Elizabeth. *Blow Ye Winds Westerly: The Seaports and Sailing Ships of Old New England.* Harper, 1972.

Goldstein, Peggy. *Long Is a Dragon: Chinese Writing for Children.* China Books and Periodicals, Inc., 1991.

Haufrecht, Herbert. *The Laura Ingalls Wilder Songbook.* Harper and Row, 1968.

Jackson, Joseph Henry. *Bad Company.* University of Nebraska Press, 1949.

Lake, A. I. *Gold Fever.* Rourke Publications, 1990.

Levine, Ellen. *If You Traveled West by Covered Wagon.* Scholastic Books, 1986.

Lyngheim, Linda M. *Gold Rush Adventure.* Langtry Pubns., 1988.

McNeer, May. *The California Gold Rush.* Landmark Books, 1977.

Pack, Janet. *California.* Watts, 1987.

Rawls, Jim. *Dame Shirley and the Gold Rush.* Steck-Vaughn Co. 1993.

Ray, H.A. *The Stars.* Houghton Mifflin, 1980.

Seidman, Laurence I. *Fools of '49.* Knopf, 1976.

Stein, R. Conrad. *The Story of the Gold at Sutter's Mill.* Childrens, 1981.

Trafzer, Clifford. *California's Indians and the Gold Rush.* Sierra Oaks Company, 1989.

Van Steenwyke, Elizabeth. *The California Gold Rush.* Franklin Watts, 1991.

Wade, Linda M. *California: The Rush for Gold.* Rourke Enterprises, 1991.

Jackdaws

Jackdaws are portfolios of historical documents. They may be ordered from Jackdaw Publications, P.O. Box 503, Amamwalk, NY 10501-503.

Answer Key

Amy's Crossword Puzzle

Work in cooperative groups to solve this puzzle
Go for the Gold! Can your group complete the puzzle first?
Check answers together.

```
³S P A N I S H
 H
¹V A Q U E R O S
 R
 R        ¹L        ²C          ⁴F
 ⁴N E W Y E A R S D A Y        R
 O        V        L          A
          I   ⁶C A L I F O R N I O S
 ²N U ⁶G G E T   F   ⁸S O M B R E R O ⁷S
   O L       ⁵S A N F R A N C I S C O  T
   O F       R   U              R      R
   D R       U   S              E      E
   F E       ⁹F A R M E R              A
   E V       ⁷S H I P          E       M
   V E                         A
   E R              ¹⁰J O H N S U T T E R
   R               ¹¹S A R A P E S
```

Across

1. "Cowboys" in California
2. What Amy found in the stream
3. Language spoken by most people in California in 1848
4. When Amy began her diary
5. Where Amy's family moved when they left the farm
6. Mexican people who remained in California after the war with the United States
7. What Amy's father bought in San Francisco
8. Broad-brimmed hats worn by vaqueros
9. What Amy's father did for a living
10. Important person expected for New Year's dinner

Down

1. Famous tailor the Harrises met in San Francisco
2. Place where Amy and her family lived
3. Amy's older sister
4. Amy's younger sister
5. Long ropes or lassos
6. Wanting gold so much that becomes a sickness

Gold Country Map

By the Great Hornspoon!

Trace the movements of Jack and Praiseworthy from San Francisco through the gold country and back to San Francisco.

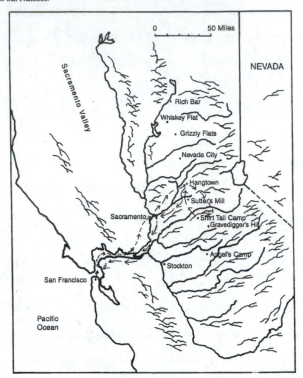

Gold Rush Math

Forty-Niners worked hard to pan their gold out of California streams, and they needed sharp math skills to exchange their gold correctly for the things they needed.

Keep your math skills as sharp as a Forty-Niner's.

Solve these puzzles:

Add the numbers in each row and column and along each diagonal. Also, add the numbers in each of the four corners. Each of the sums must equal 34.

16	2	3	13
5	11	10	8
9	7	6	12
4	14	15	1

7	2	11	14
6	15	10	3
12	1	8	13
9	16	5	4

Complete each of these grids so that there are subtraction facts across and down.

8	−	4	=	4
−	Gold	−	⚒	−
5	−	2	=	3
=	⚒	=	Fever	=
3	−	2	=	1

14	−	5	=	9
−	California	−	🛒	−
7	−	3	=	4
=	⚖	=	or Bust!	=
7	−	2	=	5